Quantitative Economic Research:
Trends and Problems

NATIONAL BUREAU OF ECONOMIC RESEARCH

General Series 96

Economic Research: Retrospect and Prospect

Quantitative Economic Research: Trends and Problems

Fiftieth Anniversary Colloquium VII

by

SIMON KUZNETS

Harvard University

NATIONAL BUREAU OF ECONOMIC RESEARCH
NEW YORK 1972

Distributed by COLUMBIA UNIVERSITY PRESS
NEW YORK AND LONDON

Relation of National Bureau Directors to Publications
Reporting Proceedings of the Fiftieth Anniversary Colloquia

Since the present volume is a record of colloquium proceedings, it has
been exempted from the rules governing submission of manuscripts to,
and critical review by, the Board of Directors of the National Bureau.
(Resolution adopted July 6, 1948, as revised
November 21, 1949, and April 20, 1968)

Fiftieth Anniversary Colloquium Series

To commemorate its fiftieth anniversary the National Bureau of Economic Research sponsored a series of colloquia to explore the effects of pending and anticipated policy issues on future research priorities for areas of long-standing Bureau concern. As a basis for the panel and audience discussions, economists specializing in the subject area prepared papers in which they reviewed relevant research advances through time and presented their opinions for the direction of future effort. These papers, and in some instances edited transcripts of panelists' comments, appear as part of the National Bureau's Fiftieth Anniversary publications series. Papers developed for the colloquia and publications series and participants in the program included:

THE BUSINESS CYCLE TODAY
September 24, 1970—New York City

Moderators:
>   Morning session: Paul A. Samuelson
>   Afternoon session: F. Thomas Juster

Presentations:
>   "Dating American Growth Cycles" *Ilse Mintz*
>   "The 'Recession' of 1969–1970" *Solomon Fabricant*
>   "The Cyclical Behavior of Prices" *Geoffrey H. Moore*
>   "Forecasting Economic Conditions: The Record and the Prospect"
>   *Victor Zarnowitz*
>   "Econometric Model Simulations and the Cyclical Characteristics
>   of the U.S. Economy" *Victor Zarnowitz*
>   "A Study of Discretionary and Nondiscretionary Monetary and
>   Fiscal Policies in the Context of Stochastic Macroeconometric
>   Models" *Yoel Haitovsky and Neil Wallace*

Panelists:
  Morning session: Otto Eckstein, Henry C. Wallich
  Afternoon session: Bert G. Hickman, Arthur M. Okun

FINANCE AND CAPITAL MARKETS
October 22, 1970—New York City

Moderator: Robert V. Roosa

Presentation:
  "Finance and Capital Markets"   *John Lintner*

Panelists: William J. Baumol, Sidney Homer, James J. O'Leary

A ROUNDTABLE ON POLICY ISSUES AND RESEARCH OPPORTUNITIES IN INDUSTRIAL ORGANIZATION
November 5, 1970—Chicago, Illinois

Moderator: Victor R. Fuchs

Presentations:
  "Industrial Organization: Boxing the Compass"
                                      James W. McKie
  "Antitrust Enforcement and the Modern Corporation"
                                      Oliver E. Williamson
  "Issues in the Study of Industrial Organization in a Regime of Rapid
    Technical Change"   *Richard R. Nelson*
  "Industrial Organization: A Proposal for Research"
                                      Ronald H. Coase

PUBLIC EXPENDITURES AND TAXATION
December 2, 1970—Washington, D.C.

Moderator: Walter W. Heller

Presentation:
"Quantitative Research in Taxation and Government Expenditure"
Carl S. Shoup

Panelists: James M. Buchanan, Richard R. Musgrave

ECONOMIC GROWTH
December 10, 1970—San Francisco, California

Moderator: R. Aaron Gordon

Presentation:
"Is Growth Obsolete?"
William D. Nordhaus and James Tobin

Panelists: Moses Abramovitz, Robin C. O. Matthews

HUMAN RESOURCES
May 13, 1971—Atlanta, Georgia

Moderator: Gary S. Becker

Presentation:
"Human Capital: Policy Issues and Research Opportunities"
Theodore W. Schultz

Panelists: Alice M. Rivlin, Gerald S. Somers

THE FUTURE OF ECONOMIC RESEARCH
April 23, 1971—South Brookline, Massachusetts

Presentation:
"Quantitative Economic Research: Trends and Problems"

Simon Kuznets

Contents

Foreword

In this paper I refrain from reviewing the past quantitative research at the National Bureau of Economic Research on the broader aspects of this country's economy —a task too great for a single scholar, and one that I would hesitate to undertake because my active participation in that work over some thirty-five years might detract from my objectivity. The discussion here is, rather, a series of broad judgments on conditions of quantitative economic research and on its trends in this country—judgments that still reflect a set of personal views and observations, backed, it is hoped, by sufficient illustration to provide a useful, noneccentric basis for discussion of needed research and of the possible role of the National Bureau.

In formulating these observations and judgments, it was clearly impossible to escape the criteria that guided my own research and the influence of my own experience. But the discussion is presented in the hope that it will gain a critical review, and generate alternative judgments and criteria in their bearing on the National Bureau's research program.

I have profited from comments made in a discussion of an earlier version of this paper by Jagdish Bhagwati, Robert Gordon, Christopher Sims, and Theodore W. Schultz. As always, I am indebted to Lillian Weksler for a thorough editing.

SIMON KUZNETS
Cambridge, Mass.

Introduction

Economists everywhere know Simon Kuznets for his contributions to their science. Business cycles, seasonal variations in industry and trade, national income and its distribution, capital and capital formation, economic growth—each of these subjects, in turn, and others as well, "has been the object of Kuznets' attention, and each has been shaken and advanced by some fresh and penetrating study. To few men is it given to make a truly significant difference in the state of a science, but Kuznets did it more than once." [1] In quantitative economic research he is, indeed, the outstanding figure of our generation. The reflections he offers here on trends and problems in his field of scientific endeavor are therefore sure to command the attention of his professional colleagues.

Others may be led to join Kuznets' audience by the news of the award to him of the 1971 Nobel Prize in Economic Science. For them, a few additional remarks by way of introduction may be appropriate. First, then, on the occasion of Kuznets' paper.

The National Bureau was founded, half a century ago, for the objective determination and impartial interpretation of the facts bearing upon important economic problems. There must have been real questions at the time whether this standard could be met and, equally essential, whether the Bureau's findings could be made to "carry conviction to all thoughtful men, however divergent their views of public policy." Yet the Bureau's

[1] Moses Abramovitz in *Science,* October 29, 1971.

statement of principles, from which I have been quoting, boldly declared these to be the aims of the new venture.

That the Bureau did succeed in attaining its high objectives is clear. It is evidenced by the wide use made of the long list of Bureau studies by persons with diverse views on policy. It is evidenced also by the Bureau's ability to enlist growing support for its work from a wide variety of sources. In this accomplishment the many distinguished persons who gathered together at the Bureau's fiftieth anniversary meetings saw cause enough for celebration. Coming at a time, as Kuznets observes, when despair concerning "the relevance of reasoned and objective discourse to the solution of social problems" is apparently spreading, their participation in the anniversary meetings constituted a declaration of faith in the purposes and uses of objective economic research. And it constituted also a tribute to the Bureau's founders, the men who set its goals and designed the organization under which the goals could be brought within reach, the men who set an enduring example, in their objectivity, standards of workmanship, and willingness to reason together, for all who came after them.

The Bureau's fiftieth anniversary was also an occasion for looking ahead. This was a major purpose of the colloquia, listed elsewhere in this volume, in one of which Kuznets presented his paper on quantitative economic research.

But why single out quantitative research? There is a place in all scientific undertaking for theoretical speculation. In the end, however, theory must be made to stand up to the test of conformity with experience or experiment. As Kuznets underlines, it is only *tested* theory that can carry conviction; it is only tested theory

xvi

that can provide the solid ground in which sound policy must be rooted. To be useful, then, economic research must be empirically oriented.

But this is not sufficient. The choice among economic policies always means weighing alternatives. And weighing alternatives requires determining the net balance between forces working in opposite directions. Estimates must be made of the strength of these forces, and of the magnitudes and timing of their direct and indirect effects. To be of more than minimal value, objective economic knowledge must be quantitative in character.

That is why the National Bureau has concentrated its efforts on quantitative economic research. It is for this reason also that, in planning the discussion of its future work, a broad survey of trends and problems in quantitative economic research seemed eminently suitable for one of the Bureau's anniversary colloquia.

As might be expected of an economist who has made major advances in the design and use of economic measures, Kuznets has a good deal to say about these measures and about the statistical data on which they are based. Particularly, he emphasizes the dependence of economic measures upon the social philosophy of the time and place to which they refer. It is especially noteworthy, at a time when the usefulness of such measurements as GNP is in question, that Kuznets has always recognized this dependence. His discussion is not a belated response to the current wave of criticism. The National Bureau's assessment and reassessment of measures of economic and social performance now under way are within a tradition established at the Bureau decades ago.

Also noteworthy is Kuznets' judgment that in far too few of the econometric studies now flourishing is sufficient attention devoted to the quality of the statistics fitted into the equations. His insistence that truly scientific quantitative economic research requires a more critical use of the statistics may serve to give pause to econometricians. Required also, in his view, is that they should go beyond the readily available statistics; a larger fraction of their resources should be used to dig up more of the basic material they will process. As important is Kuznets' opinion that econometricians could be more mindful than many of them are of the extent to which their results are influenced by the assumptions they build into their equations.

Kuznets is not content to speak of quantitative economic research in general terms. He illustrates many of his points by reference to the particular subject of economic growth. This is the subject to which he has devoted most of the past two decades and for which he was especially cited by the Swedish Academy. It is therefore not surprising that he should stress its importance and go on to suggest that the National Bureau might seriously consider building its program of research around economic growth as the central theme.

Economic growth has always been a major area of research at the National Bureau. In its very first study, of national income in the United States, one of the objectives was to learn something about the long-term rate of growth. Many subsequent studies at the National Bureau —Kuznets' own study of *National Product Since 1869* and his *Capital in the American Economy*—are outstanding examples, and there are also the National Bureau's studies on mechanization, productivity, employment, and production—all aimed especially at economic growth. In addition, many of the Bureau's other studies, human

capital, for example, have in large or small degree contributed to the knowledge being accumulated on the
economic growth of the United States.

Kuznets is not alone in stressing economic growth as
a subject for the National Bureau's program. Many of
the suggestions on the Bureau's future program made
in the other colloquia bear on subjects closely related to
economic growth. The fifth colloquium, of course, concentrated on this subject. And a major theme of the first
colloquium, *The Business Cycle Today,* was the shift in
concept of business cycles from the older idea of an
absolute up and down movement in output, employment,
and other economic quantities to one of fluctuations in
rates of growth.

No doubt, then, economic growth will continue to be
a major area of research at the National Bureau. Whether
the time is ripe for making it the central theme, as Kuznets believes, is a question that will be given serious attention, along with other questions on the Bureau's program raised in the various colloquia.

Kuznets suggests, further, that the study of economic
growth might best be pursued on a comparative international basis. The possibility is intriguing in a world in
which concern with the economic status of fellow human
beings abroad is greater than ever before. But, as he goes
on to say in his paper, the data for most countries still
leave very much to be desired. To develop anything even
approximating the quantity and quality of information
for other countries that has been developed for the
United States would be a task far beyond the resources
of any single research institute now in existence. What
may turn out to be most practicable is a cooperative
arrangement among institutes of various countries. An

effort along this line—a study of the diffusion of new technologies—is now being tried by the Bureau. Experience to date with this and other cooperative ventures on an international basis makes for some optimism about the possibility.

*   *   *   *   *

The human affairs that economists study are important: the quantity of goods and services produced and consumed—their quality, rate of growth, stability, and distribution among the people; the conditions and opportunities of life and of work—how the standard of living is affected by the size of population and how the population is affected by the standard of living; under what social and political arrangements "the ordinary business of life" is best carried out. These and other economic questions have deeply concerned men for centuries. To cast light on these questions economists devote their hours and their years to research. They hope in this way to make economic policies better than they would otherwise be—policies that men are impelled to try, in their persistent efforts to raise economic welfare.

"Much has surely been learned; a vast stock of relevant economic measures has accumulated; the inventory of relatively firm empirical findings has grown; and a host of theoretical hypotheses has been advanced. . . ." But Kuznets hastens to add to this judgment significant caveats. Many of these hypotheses are "too simple and partial to be valid without major and, short of wider study, unspecifiable qualifications. . . . We are still far from a tested theory of economic growth. . . . Many questions remain that demand intensive exploration and at least provisional answers as necessary elements even in a tentative understanding of the growth process." The remarkable postwar record of successful economic performance, Kuznets observes, "is not necessarily evidence that we understand the process. . . . Paradoxically, the number of questions and the variety of what may be seen as policy problems may be greater . . . than in the 'good old' days when both study and growth were relatively stagnant, economic growth was viewed as a process much beyond the control of man, and its low rate did not produce the unsettling impact of rapid structural changes."

There is much to be done. Difficult questions plague us—questions on economic growth, and also on business cycles, finance and capital markets, industrial organization, public expenditures and taxation, and human resources, to list the subjects of the National Bureau's colloquia. Kuznets' observations on trends and problems in the field of quantitative economic research should help economists working on any of these subjects. And they should help economists working under any auspices, in the tasks they tackle. But Kuznets sees the responsibilities and opportunities of economists working together in nongovernmental public research institutes to be especially great. This kind of institution, he says, "is not only a research laboratory for the specialist, but also in a way a finder and keeper of truth for society at large; a producer of tested and acceptable measures, and a source of the balanced evaluation and judgment that should facilitate social consensus." If Kuznets is right in this judgment, the opportunities open to the National Bureau in the half-century ahead are not less attractive than those of the past half-century; and the responsibilities entailed, not less worth shouldering than those the Bureau assumed half a century ago.

SOLOMON FABRICANT
New York University
and National Bureau of
Economic Research

Quantitative Economic Research:
Trends and Problems

1. EMPHASIS ON THE NATIONAL ECONOMY

Much of the work of the National Bureau has been either on aggregative or on more specialized aspects of the national economy of this country. This is true of the studies of national income and wealth, capital formation, productivity, consumption, economic growth, and business cycles, which account for a predominant proportion of the Bureau studies. The same concentration on the economies of units classifiable as sovereign states characterizes all economic research—if we define it as the systematic use of observational data aimed at findings of established relevance to economic analysis. Here economic analysis is taken to be the implicit analysis typical of economic history, or the formalized structure of economic theory, or the combination of history and theory that provides intellectual bases for consideration of economic policy. Even when regions or components within the national economy are stressed, reference to the national aggregate must provide the weights and reveal the role of the region or component which is an integral part of the aggregate. Even when larger groupings of, or relations among, national economies are emphasized, the basic unit is still the national economy, as may be seen in any international compendium of statistics or in studies on international relations and comparative economic growth and structure.

The reasons for this concentration on, and persistent reference to, the national economy are far-reaching. The foremost reason is that the sovereign state sets the institutional conditions within which economic ac-

1

tivities are pursued, the boundaries within which markets operate and within which human resources are relatively free to handle material capital assets and claims to them. Furthermore, given the continuously changing material technology generally characteristic of countries taking advantage of modern economic growth potentials, the sovereign government is the overriding authority that resolves conflicts generated by growth and screens institutional innovations, sanctioning those believed essential and barring others. Except for such recent, and still incomplete, unions like the European Common Market, no combination of two or more sovereign states can be treated as a single source for basic decisions that channel economic performance or that resolve the internal conflicts generated by economic growth and related social change. Such a treatment would face major difficulties: limited mobility of resources, restricted freedom to pursue divergent paths of social innovation, and absence of community of feeling, among others.

It is the existence of national economies, separated from the rest of the world by, and unified under, the aegis of an effective sovereign government, and yet large and internally diverse enough to comprise distinct social and economic groups, that may have led to what is perhaps the most pervasive idea in economics. This is the conception of an economy as a system of different but interrelated parts, a system that is a unit despite the differences in its component elements and its partial dependence on other such units in the world. To be sure, this concept could be applied to a firm, or a region, or the world. But in the former two cases, there is little basis for claiming that the system is so independent of

2

others that it constitutes a separate unit susceptible of complete analysis; and in the case of the world, one can hardly argue that the national economies are integral parts of a unified system. It could be claimed that the notion of society in pre-Classical economics was even more representative of a unified system of diverse parts, in suggesting that the several economic and social groups, although different, were interrelated and analogous to the several members of the human body. But it was the great contribution of the discipline of economics to deny that the diversity within the society was innate in human nature or in blood lines, but was, rather, limited to differences in economic functions—which left the individual free to seek that function for which he felt most suited.

Without committing myself to an adequate exploration of the sources of the basic economic concept suggested above, I merely suggest that this concept of an economy represents a stylized reflection of the unity in diversity, of cooperation through the markets as set by an effective central authority, that might prevail within national economies under the aegis of a viable sovereign government. The economy is seen as a unified system of interdependent components, with members capable of responding to the market impulses in a forecastable (and under certain conditions, optimal) way.

If a national economy is the most likely empirical counterpart of the major notion of economic analysis, and if economic research aims at findings relevant to economic analysis, it follows that economic research must concentrate on national economies—their aggregate dimensions, their component parts, and the interrelations of the latter. This connection is strengthened

3

when we consider the bearing of economic research and analysis on national policy. If the sovereign state is the major agency entrusted by society to set the rules, to define the institutional channels for economic and social behavior, the major practical use of economic analysis, whether in history or theory, and of the research relevant to such analysis, is in translating the findings into some policy choices, with alternatives available to the sovereign government. In the evolution of modern economies, much economic analysis was generated by the presumption that the problematical and undesirable consequences of the operation of the economy could be avoided or minimized, without undue loss, by modifications of the rules or by some other ameliorative action within the purview of the authoritative organs of society—a major responsibility of such authority. Since the sovereign state constitutes that authority, the conception of its responsibilities vis-à-vis the economy leads naturally to concentration of economic analysis on the national economy. This argument, while similar to the one made above, is new in that it stresses the importance of our *views* on the feasible role of the government, since any changes in these views mean changes in the volume and direction of economic research.

Concentration on national economies, with due regard to the major distinct but interrelated sectors and components, still leaves wide scope for economic research. And, indeed, a glance at the many accepted specialties and "fields" in the discipline of economics reveals differences in emphasis on production sectors (agriculture, industry, transportation, etc.); on production factors (labor, capital); on infrastructure institutions, particu-

4

larly those dealing with money and credit; on regulatory
agencies and government in all the variety of its drafts
upon and contributions to the economy; and on international flows (including the economics of war and defense). All of this is in addition to the pursuit of the
total view of the national economy in history and theory,
including quantitative history and quantitative tests of
formally structured concepts and hypotheses. Obviously
one man cannot deal with trends and prospects in economic research in all of these broad fields. Some have
already been covered in the six colloquia organized by
the National Bureau, which provide us with some general insights that will be touched upon below.[1] I, therefore, limit my discussion to *quantitative* or *statistical*
economic research concentrated on the broadest aspects
of the national economy. Even this field is so wide that
it permits only impressions that will necessarily reflect
my own experience and intellectual predilections. However, they may be useful as bases for discussion of the
major priorities in quantitative economic research in this
country, with possible inferences for the program of the
National Bureau.

Because economic analysis concentrates on the national economy, the research, which is the empirical
counterpart of, and basis for, economic analysis, demands the statistical approach (thus emphasizing again
the original meaning of statistics as the study of quantitative aspects of states, i.e., of nations). In thought-
experiments, which constitute much of economic theory,
one can operate with a typical or representative unit—

[1] See pp. vii–x for a description of these colloquia.

5

economic man, the business firm, the demander, the supplier, the unit of labor, the unit of capital, etc.—and the behavioral pattern of each unit as a formalized reflection of the actual behavior of real members of economic society. With the addition of a few exogenous assumptions (hopefully realistic), one can derive some interesting conclusions as to the functioning of an economy. These exercises are valuable in demonstrating how the social phenomenon of the market, and of market-determined output and its allocation, emerges from the activities of numerous individual units in rational response to economic motives. They may also be useful in deriving some secular trends, with the help of plausible exogenous assumptions concerning natural resource supplies, technology, and the like. But the difficulty is that representative firms in agriculture differ substantially in size, responsiveness, etc., from representative firms in industry or in trade; and that the impact of behavioral patterns on various parts of the economy changes with advances in technology, changing requirements for material or human capital, and so forth. Since the outcome of formalized reasoning concerning the combined effects of representative firms or units depends upon the weights of the differing groups and the rate and direction of impacts of changes in technology and correlated social innovations, we need statistical measures of these factors. Furthermore, the exogenous factors embodied in the assumption may change significantly over time, and in directions different from those postulated in the assumption—obvious examples being the changes from the demographic patterns assumed in the Malthusian set of Classical (and implicitly Marxian) economics, and, even more, the striking effect of technological power vis-à-vis

6

exhaustion of natural resources, the latter of major concern in the late eighteenth and much of nineteenth century economics. The *complexity* of national economies, with their diverse parts, makes quantification indispensable. The incidence of rapid *shifts* in weights (structure) and of movements in total productivity makes continuous statistical observation imperative. And the changing *social* processes, so closely related to the economic, may necessitate continuous extension of quantitative economic research to aspects of society with which the economic discipline is not currently concerned.

We can now consider some specific aspects of the task of quantitative economic research, concentrated on the national economy and directed at findings explicitly related to economic analysis—whether for history, theory, or policy. These aspects reflect the conditions under which quantitative economic research is pursued—conditions with reference to the supply of data and, to some extent, of human resources, in relation to the requirements of economic analysis.

2. CONDITIONS OF QUANTITATIVE RESEARCH

The Supply of Primary Data

The main fact of life in quantitative research on the national economy is that the supply of primary data is beyond the direct intellectual control of the scholar, in his individual or collective capacity. An economist, unlike a scholar in the experimental natural sciences, cannot isolate "pure" cases of economic and social activity on a countrywide scale. He can only simulate, by la-

7

boriously transforming a huge volume of primary data, which have not been collected by him or his laboratory assistants, or at his command. His observational measurements differ from those of scientists in an observational natural science like astronomy in which measurements are based on primary data specially collected for the scholar, under his control, and derived by means of tools specially designed in response to questions posed within the discipline. Most of the primary data in economics are supplied by the economic units, acting in their individual capacity or for the economic firms and agencies. Even when data collection does not depend on the knowledge and response of the subject under observation, such huge costs are involved for the national economy that the task is beyond the capacity of individual scholars or even academic and research institutions. And, since the market for primary economic data is limited and discontinuous, profit-oriented business firms are not interested in providing them, except occasionally for some narrowly defined information on consumer demand and the like. As a result, the sovereign government and its administrative and statistical agencies are the main suppliers of primary data relating to the national economy, which they collect largely from individuals and firms, either in the course of administration or for the specific purpose of securing socially necessary information concerning the performance of the economy and society.

The primary data on national economies represent preponderantly information provided by individuals, firms, and agencies on their own characteristics and activities; and are collected, processed, and made available largely by governments. The knowledge possessed by individuals, business firms, and public agencies about their

8

own characteristics and activities (sometimes assembled only in response to questions put by authority) differs widely in scope and quality. It depends upon the level of economic and social development, which determines the extent of quantification imposed by the very conditions of life and work. The willingness to provide such knowledge to an outside agency, even the authoritative government, also varies in space and time, depending upon the relation between people and government. The choices by governments of what may be considered socially necessary data may also differ in space and time. The data must warrant the effort to impose upon people the obligation to provide the information and the cost of collecting and processing it; and both such costs and the value of the returns may vary in space and change over time. Another variable is the readiness of the governments to publish the data in a form that would facilitate objective analysis, or to publish them at all.

The resulting differences in the scope and quality of primary data bear *some* relation to the needs of research directed at economic analysis. After all, some of the major problems dealt with by the latter may also be considered major by the country's authoritative agencies, and thus the collection and assembly of some relevant primary data may result. But even then there may be long lags between the identification of the problem in economic analysis, the acknowledgment of its usefulness as a guide to government action, and the collection of primary data relating to it. Furthermore, the concern of economic analysis with a specific problem bears no inherent relation to the ability to secure the necessary reliable primary data. For example, we are at present greatly concerned with the problems of the less developed countries. In contrast with the data-rich developed countries, the supply of data for the less developed countries is still extremely meager, and much of it is of poor quality. Another example is the problem faced in the analysis of some sectors in a developed country: the paucity of reliable data on output (as distinct from input) of major sectors of service industries does not lessen the interest of economic research in them. A third illustration is the concern of economic research with the economic performance in the Communist countries, a concern which continues despite the data blackouts and other policies that limit the supply of significant information for scholarly analysis.

Several consequences follow. First, at any given time, economic research is bound by the limitations of the supply of primary data, the gaps in their coverage, and the poor quality of some of them. Some of these limitations can be overcome by exercising ingenuity in deriving approximations; and much of the effort of economic research is, in fact, invested in bridging the gaps between the primary data and the measures required by the analytical work of the discipline (of which more below). The limitations of data supply must be recognized; and it must be emphasized that the resulting measures are only approximations and should be treated as such. Moreover, it must be realized that only untested conjectures on some important problems in economic research are possible at any given time.

Second, in the longer run, the research economist can have a marked influence on the supply of primary data, for his analysis can indicate the magnitude of the problem to which the lacking data are relevant, as well as the least costly devices by which such data can be se-

10

cured. By demonstrating the socially necessary character of the missing data, he can raise the probability of their inclusion in the statistical programs of the government agencies. The substantive use of economic research to point up a problem, and stress the gap in data supply, is an important prerequisite for improvement in the supply of primary data. Over the long period from the Classical school through the first quarter of the twentieth century, the failure of economic analysis to employ observational data, particularly statistics, on an extensive and systematic basis was partly responsible for the deficiencies in the supply of data relevant to many key problems. It also contributed to conspicuous errors in the long-term projections of the Classical and Marxian schools, with a consequent neglect of economic growth problems until a few decades back.

Third, because the supply of primary data frequently lags behind the emergence of problems requiring economic analysis, there is a tendency toward a succession of explosive expansions of analysis and findings that shift from one complex of problems to another. On the one hand, the emergence of economic problems unforeseen and unexplained by prior knowledge (of which more below) mobilizes whatever little analysis can be brought to bear on the problems. On the other hand, the supply of data, once mustered for the task, if with some delay, provides the empirical base for a more testable analysis of the problem. As time passes, and some adjustment to the problem is made by analysis and policy, it tends to recede from the forefront of economic research, although many questions may remain unanswered. It recedes because new problems, new "surprises," emerge and shift

11

the focus of preoccupation of economic analysis and research elsewhere.

Fourth, given the propensity to long swings in the focus of economic research—for example, from problems of monopoly and industrial organization to those of labor; from those of depressions to those of wars; from those of economic growth to those of urban agglomeration and inequalities in income distribution— the capacity of economic analysis to handle them depends upon a continuously available framework. This framework should help to place each problem in its proper setting and might constitute a scheme, the empirical counterpart of which could be a guide to the accumulation and organization of data and the provision of an increasingly effective basis for handling a succession of new problems. One great advantage of an aggregative statistical framework like national economic accounts (preferably with its several variants, including input-output, and covering the flows not only of output but also of labor and capital) is that it calls for a *comprehensive* and properly *articulated* (sectored) view of the whole economy. It prevents undue emphasis on any one current problem in isolation from, and neglect of, the rest of the economy; and it reveals the gaps in the data relating to all aspects and sectors, and thus is a guide for the improvement in data supply. Deplorably thin as the economic accounts may be at any given time, they provide the only empirical basis for tackling a new problem. Since national economic accounts are the empirical counterpart of the conceptual framework, of the basic notions of economic analysis, all we are saying is that an analytical framework—a well-defined view of the economy and of its relevant components in the form

12

of an empirically translatable system—provides the basis for continuity and direction of economic research and analysis, which are constantly being buffeted by the urgent problems of the moment.

From Primary Data to Economic Measures

Even assuming complete and reliable primary data on the national economy, a major task remains: to translate the data into economic measures, i.e., magnitudes corresponding to the clearly defined economic concepts used in economic analysis. A firm can submit a detailed record of its economic activity—the purchases of inputs (materials, labor, etc.) in quantities and prices, the volume of output, the sales in quantities and prices, etc. But all this is only raw material for a key economic concept like net output, or the productive factors involved; and thorny questions arise in converting such raw material into a finished economic measure. The economic analyst must decide whether all the payments of the firm which are treated as costs represent inputs and must be subtracted (e.g., payments of taxes); what productive factors are represented by some payments of income (e.g., the net income of the individual, unincorporated entrepreneur); whether the firm has, in addition to reporting its private costs, made allowance for social costs (e.g., land depletion in the case of farming, effect on environment in the case of the industrial plant), and hence whether its net output is the proper net; and whether the prices of inputs and outputs provide the proper weights (some may be affected by subsidies or special allocations of otherwise controlled foreign exchange, or prices of inputs and outputs may relate to

13

different time periods, with effects on net income as cal-
culated by the firm).

The number, variety, and thorniness of such questions
multiply rapidly as we shift from a firm to larger groupings and finally to the national economy. The very sectoring, the grouping, is not set by the primary data that
come from the indivisible basic units within the society
and economy. The familiar set of production sectors is
a reflection of our knowledge as observers of the differences among these sectors in the raw materials used, the
production processes employed, and the product turned
out—differences that are also reflected in distinctive
groupings among persons engaged in each sector, in
their recognition of common group interests, and their
differences from other groups. But a number of criteria
of grouping are available to us; and differences between
the institutional and the more analytical types of classification are marked (distinctions among producer and
consumer goods industries, small- and large-scale sectors, competitive and monopolistic types of industries,
young and old industries, among others). In aggregating
firms into these larger groupings, the questions of identification of costs, duplication in output, disparities in
price bases, distinction of productive factors, all gain
greater importance and become more difficult to handle.
Furthermore, we face additional problems: we must set
the boundaries of the groups, decide on the treatment of
units belonging to more than one sector, and specify the
role of some sectors vis-à-vis others (e.g., of the finance
sector relative to the production sectors from which it
derives most of its income). Establishing the criteria for
sectoring and proper aggregation is obviously a major
role of economic analysis; it spells the difference between
14

summation of primary data by common-sense observational criteria, which usually reflect the group interests within the economic society, and the proper economic measures. To illustrate: the total tonnage of steel produced by the country's steel industry, excluding any hobby- or housewife-generated steel output (a negligible problem here, but of greater concern for other commodities and services) is a primary datum, the first step toward an economic measure. The *net* output of the industry is the next step; the net output of all producer goods (of which steel is partly one) is the further step; and, for many analytical purposes, the share of the net output of the producer goods sector in the national product is the relevant economic measure—a fair distance from the gross output of steel and of each of the other producer goods expressed in their diverse quantities.

The variety and scope of the questions just illustrated are at their greatest in connection with measures relating to the total economy—not only the customary measures of national product and its components, but also the related totals of labor force and employment, capital stock, the price level and the money supply, size distributions of income, and the like. To use the most familiar illustration, with national product or income totals viewed as properly weighted combinations of different components, we find that the major questions relate to: (1) the boundaries between economic activity and life in general (which latter may yield "products" of its own), and between market-oriented "outputs" and resulting "incomes," which should be excluded because they do not reflect any productive contribution (problems of scope, or inclusion and exclusion); (2) the definitions of inputs and output, which are needed to avoid duplication and, in particular,

15

to record hidden costs in order to exclude what appear to be net returns but are merely offsets to increases in the cost of living, these increases, in turn, being due to changes in conditions *imposed* by the new technology that augments gross output (problems of grossness and netness, or final and intermediate products); (3) the weights (prices) by which the net outputs, once properly defined, are to be combined into a meaningful total, the magnitude of which is a reliable gauge of aggregate net change.[2]

These problems vary in form (appearance, rather than substance) with the method used to approximate nation-wide net output at different levels. The problems involved in reducing gross output to net output within each production sector by estimating purchases from other sectors and internal capital consumption differ from those involved in estimating returns to productive factors (the latter properly identified and the former properly defined) within the several productive sectors distinguished; and these differ from those faced in measuring the flow of finished product into final uses (including inventories as part of capital formation). Other groups of questions arise when different types of sectoring are considered. One of the most productive of additional problems is the distinction within inputs and outputs between domestic origin and flow from abroad; another is the distribution of income among groups within the population, distinguished by size of income or by some other economic or social characteristic. Similar questions, regarding boundaries and internal weighting, if not dupli-

[2] For a detailed discussion, see Simon Kuznets, *National Income and Its Composition,* New York, National Bureau of Economic Research, 1941, pp. 3–60.

16

cation, arise when we consider stocks of productive factors, such as labor force and capital, or price indexes of different coverage. And there is the obvious corollary that the answer to the questions, for national product, for nationwide stocks of labor and capital (or for output and productive factors within separate sectors), or for prices, must be consistent if the resulting economic measures are to be unequivocal contributions to economic analysis.

That the conversion of primary economic data into economic measures requires answers to problems like those just indicated, has widespread effects on quantitative economic research. To illustrate we again use the problems connected with national product measurement. Some questions involve the definition of economic activity, the very boundaries of the economic discipline. Others involve the distinction between productive and unproductive activities, with all the complexities of the differences between private and public gains, and are thus related to welfare theory. Still others call for distinctions between input and output, and involve a theory of production, a theory of input requirements that would set the conditions under which the identified inputs tend to yield the expected output, suggest the joint products that may emerge, and would also define the finished, final products that constitute ultimate output. Finally, the valuation problems clearly raise questions concerning prices as gauges of value, of major concern in the theory of value and price.

In short, such problems—and they are only of somewhat narrower scope for some major components of national output, and of a different cast but hardly less complex for some income distributions—require, on the

17

one hand, a definitive statement of the ultimate goals of economic activity, with boundaries between it and other aspects of social life clearly drawn; and, on the other, a variety of theories. These theories or analytical hypotheses are concerned with private and social welfare, the identity of productive factors and the conditions under which they contribute to output, and the significance of prices as the proper gauges of the values of inputs and outputs consistent with the other theories and goal definitions. Two different formulations of the goals of economic activity and two different combinations of theories of value, production, and welfare will yield, for one country at one time, two different sets of aggregates and components. And one set of answers, applied to different national economies or to one economy at different times, may involve basic positions and hypotheses with different degrees of validity; and hence provide approximations implying different degrees of relevance.

The implications of these statements may now be summarized briefly, but emphatically, in view of their importance for understanding what quantitative economic research is about.

First, no economic measure is *neutral,* that is, unaffected by economic theories of production, value, and welfare, and the broader social philosophy encompassing them. This may seem to be merely a matter of semantics, in that we distinguish between a primary economic datum, like the price of a pound of white bread in a working class neighborhood in Detroit, and an economic measure, like the index of the cost of living of wage earners. But the distinction is a real one: a wide variety of economic measures, particularly the aggregative measures of national product, labor force, capital

18

stock, investment and consumption, money stock, price levels, and so on through a long list (and, as already indicated, even some measures for a single firm) rest upon a conceptual framework provided by economic analysis. They are quantitative counterparts of these concepts, and, in that sense, cannot be independent of them and of the assumptions behind them.

Economic activity, like other individual or social human activities, is purposive; its results can be meaningfully measured only in relation to some clearly defined goals and in terms of costs and returns. Primary data on output in quantity units, numbers of people, units of machinery, sales, prices, and the like are raw material for such economic measures; they are absorbed into different economic measures in accordance with the concepts and premises that assign them some relevant significance. Indeed, the key importance of economic measures, and of the economic analysis to which they are related, is that they reflect a broad consensus, sharply defined in theory and vaguely perceived in practice, on the basic purposes of economic activity and on the acceptable rules and feasible ways by which such purposes are met, i.e., goods produced, and the implicit costs and returns distributed. Of course, an immensely wide and complex body of institutional detail and technical knowledge is superimposed on this basic notion of an economic society that coexists with but is separate from others, that directs its activity at a set of socially acceptable goals that may or may not be the same in other societies, and that operates within the broad constraints of technological and social knowledge and human needs. But such institutional and technical detail assumes economic meaning only when the underlying

19

institutions and sectors are viewed as part of the more general system represented by the national economy, in both its domestic and international position. Thus, economic measures for industries, regions, processes, and other aspects of economic activities are inevitably linked with the broader assumptions and theories underlying the aggregative measures relating to the national economy.

Second, although economic measures depend upon some basic assumptions as to goals of economic activity and upon theories of production, value, and welfare, they are not arbitrary. They are not arbitrary because the assumptions and the theories are not chosen arbitrarily: the assumptions presumably reflect the broad views operative within the economic societies under observation, the accepted goals of economic activity, and the accepted rules within which economic activity is channeled; and the theories are formalized reflections of relations observed in economic reality. Indeed, one might argue that limiting the choice of assumptions to those reflecting the consensus of society, and the choice of theories to those based on observable, if simplified, reality, is indispensable if any empirical counterparts are to be found and economic measurement is to be possible. It is extremely difficult to find empirical counterparts to a set of basic purposes and rules *radically* different from those prevailing—which, incidentally, may explain the weakness of empirical bases and formulations in the writings of critics who stand outside the basic framework of the economic system. An ascetic Simeon Stylites, living in the wilderness, can only deplore the material-welfare-oriented economic activity of an economically advanced society; he can hardly analyze or measure it

20

unless he can translate the economic calculus into one of cursed evil (costs) and of blessed virtue (returns). But one should not neglect the value of deviant approaches: they may reflect early perception of new elements, and be the precursors of a change in the tested and accepted consensus.

Third, given the basic assumptions and theories governing economic measurement, the findings are objective in the sense that independent analysts, using the same assumptions and theories and the entire stock of relevant primary data, should produce roughly the same findings. The findings will not be identical if the concepts are not crystal clear, in which case their application by different analysts to specific situations may be different. Moreover, since primary data are never fully adequate, further discrepancies may emerge as different analysts use their imaginations to secure approximations in different ways. But the fuzziness of the assumptions and theories, once there is agreement on their essential content, should only be marginal; and deficiencies of primary data should only subject the findings to margins of error suggested by other knowledge of the magnitudes of the data gaps.

Fourth, while the basic assumptions of economic analysis and measurement remain the same over time, and while they may be sufficiently reflective of human goals to be applicable to a variety of national economies, the rules governing the attainment of such goals through economic activity may change over time or differ in space. Both the free market economies and the authoritarian Communist countries may accept the same set of goals in terms of material welfare through greater output and more equitable distribution, etc., but their rules of operation differ greatly. And related effects on noneco-

21

nomic costs and benefits may lower the value and relevance of purely economic comparisons, which, in any case, are difficult because of differences in meaning of the value-price systems in the two sets of countries. But even if the basic assumption and acceptable rules of economic and social activity are roughly the same, marked changes or marked differences in technology and knowledge will affect the validity of the theories of production, value and prices, and welfare. With changing technology and knowledge, the theories that had indicated given types of feasible relations between inputs and output, prices, costs and returns, may no longer provide a proper guide to meaningful measurement. In fact, they may have been inadequate even under the earlier conditions, given the usual lag between the occurrence of social changes and its perception, which must reach a level, in relation to established knowledge, sufficient to produce changes in theory. The dependence of meaningful economic measures on the underlying theories implies, then, the possibility of continuous revision, as conditions of life change and an increasingly richer record reveals gaps in our knowledge (or "puzzles," to use Schultz's term) [3] —a point to which we shall return in discussing recent trends in quantitative economic research.

Economic Measurement and Economic Research

Even a complete articulated set of national product measures is, like the more qualitative descriptive data that are an indispensable complement, raw material for

[3] Theodore W. Schultz, "Human Capital: Policy Issues and Research Opportunities," in *Economic Research: Retrospect and Prospect, Vol. VI, Human Resources,* New York, National Bureau of Economic Research, 1972.

quantitative economic research. Quantitative economic research is the combination of economic measures, with inferences based on them and on relevant complementary data, that seeks to interpret, generalize, or predict economic performance. A brief comment on these three functions of economic research (interpretive, generalizing, and predictive) may clarify matters.

A statement typical of the interpretive function of economic research, presents the measures of aggregate output, at constant prices assumed to reflect the relevant weights, for a given country over a given period; it points to the associated shifts in production structure, in order to specify the loci of growth and stagnation, and thus to interpret the significance of the growth in relation to some accepted goals of economic activity; and it evaluates the record in terms of the specific conditions and disturbances that might have affected it, relative to some long-term "normal" or capacity growth level. In evaluating the system of associated changes, the interpretive function is an attempt at a *preliminary* classification and appraisal of the new, or newly recorded, or newly analyzed experience, in the light of basic assumptions on goals and rules of social life and of the broader knowledge of economic relations embodied in economic theory.

A statement typical of the generalizing function of economic research might be the familiar Engel law. That law, properly phrased, tells us that *at any given time,* within free market economies, the proportion of income spent on food (both income and food appropriately defined) declines as we shift from the lower to the higher income-per-capita (or per consuming unit) groups. The "generalization," indicating the conditions under which the statement holds, can be associated with some exo-

23

genous assumptions (demonstrable outside the economic realm) as to the characteristics of different human needs, and hence of demand for correspondingly different goods. The generalizing function of economic research is thus an attempt to distinguish the common and invariant elements at different places or different times (or both), and by thus distinguishing the invariant from the variant, and the stable and continuing from the fluctuating and transitory, to provide the basis for a clear association with the sources of economic changes or differences. Hence, it provides the basis for estimation of policy effects or for realistic prediction.

All generalizations involve implicit predictions, in the sense that, if the conditions under which the generalization is valid persist, so will the generalization. But the specification of differences in space and, particularly, of changes over time within which the generalization was found to hold, and is assumed to hold at least sufficiently to make predictions useful, is not easy. A generalization may be based on a wide variety of tested economic measures, be subject to no exceptions within the range of available data, and have behind it a highly plausible set of interconnections among economic, and between economic and social, variables. Yet the formulation, in sufficiently general and still testable terms, of the full set of limiting conditions under which the generalization was found to be valid is difficult. The additional judgment as to the possible persistence of the generalization that would warrant a realistic prediction might be viewed as almost a separate task—although in a way it is the final test of the generalization. None is complete unless the conditions of its service as a base for realistic prediction are indicated.

24

Economic research involves, for any one of the three functions, a combination of various economic measures with other more qualitative data; and "quantitative" in the description of economic research is a matter of comparative emphasis on the type of data involved. In interpretation, economic measures are combined with other data in an attempt to classify the newly measured, or remeasured, segment of economic experience, in relation either to some basic assumptions of social purposes and rules (which often lead to re-examination of the conceptual bases of the measures themselves) or to existing knowledge of the properties of various components of an economic system and the interrelations among them. In generalization, a wide variety of economic measures and of complementary data are used in an attempt to distinguish the relatively invariant from the rest, and associate both types of changes or differences with various groups of determining factors. And, of course, predictions combine the presumptively established generalizations with additional measures and related data selected as suitable bases for extrapolation.

It follows that each of these functions, and indeed every study in quantitative economic research, requires a mixture of economic measures and other qualitative but observational data, and a range of past generalizations and hypotheses that provide the context within which new interpretations, or new generalizations, or new predictions can be made. There is no such thing in economic research as a *simple fact,* meaning an economic measure independent of basic assumptions and extant hypotheses; nor is there pure description or measurement, meaning a portrayal of economic events in terms of simple facts as just defined; nor mere accumulation

25

of facts without theory, meaning a listing of these simple facts. The basic assumptions with respect to goals of economic activity and accepted rules within which economic activity is channeled, if not always precisely stated, are clearly implicit in the measures used; and any new experience can, after adequate interpretation and evaluation, stimulate re-examination of past definitions and measurement conventions. The theoretical hypotheses concerning relations of inputs and outputs, prices, etc. may be formulated broadly, but they are clearly involved. Their formal embodiment into a system of equations, fitted to a limited stretch of observable and measured economic experience, does not represent a generalization, but only another type of interpretation, of preliminary classification, with reference to a set of hypotheses more formally, and hence more narrowly, defined. In short, there is a mixture of basic assumptions, theoretical hypotheses, economic measures, and observable qualitative evidence in all three functions of economic research, in all quantitative economic research.

Needless to say, economic research studies differ in emphasis. But one should note the preponderance in resources involved and possibly in terms of results—although reduction to comparable units is difficult—of the interpretive type of economic research. The reasons are obvious. To truly test a generalization involves a supply of primary data and economic measures that, in its coverage of relevant conditions sufficiently different to test for significant invariance, is prohibitively demanding. And most empirical generalizations for which an analytical basis has been easily formulated (there is no difficulty in generating a wide variety of plausible hypotheses) have proved, in fact, to be based on so limited

26

a universe that exceptions are all too readily observed (which applies to the Engel law and to many other such generalizations). This means that most "predictions" are on equally shaky ground, useful as they may be as a substitute for complete ignorance or for too capricious a choice of parameters for policy consideration. In view of the changeable and variegated economic universe with which empirical and quantitative research has to deal, there is natural reluctance to orient investigation directly to the ambitious task of establishing generalizations or making predictions.

To attempt empirical research in order to *test* theoretical hypotheses that result from thought-experiments is hardly sensible. These hypotheses formulate rules of behavior of individuals and firms, identify and classify productive factors, types of technological change, and the like, to provide enormously enlightening demonstrations in which socioeconomic performance, or change, or fluctuation, can be derived from the rationally expected action of the numerous members of economic society, tied usually through the market. But unless closely linked to successive levels of economic measurement, hardly feasible until recently and difficult even today, such hypotheses can only suggest how economic change or performance is *possible* under highly simplified conditions, not how the results are shaped in testable magnitudes that permit distinction between the common and the differing elements. If the thought-experiments yield some measurable concepts and classifications, it is interpretive economic research studies that use the economic measures based on these concepts and classifications, in the attempt to evaluate and interpret a stretch of economic experience. It is by means of such studies, and often with the help of a modified and more precise definition of the concepts, that interpretive economic research does in fact test the relevance of the concepts and of the presumptive relations among the elements represented by the concepts. But the intention is to use, not to test, the established concepts and underlying assumptions in interpreting new or newly measured experience. The result may be a re-evaluation of the underlying concepts and theories. It is the interpretive economic research of recent decades that led to questioning of the concepts of material capital and undifferentiated labor as the key productive factors, and stimulated the great interest in investment of human capital (the field surveyed in the Schultz paper mentioned earlier) and in the disaggregation of material capital in terms of vintages.

Given the rapid changes in economic processes and structures and the dependence of these processes, viewed in the longer run, on social and technological concomitants, it is hardly surprising that the interpretive function of economic research predominates. It employs assumptions and theoretical concepts that are sufficiently broad to permit adequate variability in institutional and technological innovations, and to leave the analysis free to question the basic premises of the measures, the classifications of factors, the distinction of production sectors, the treatment of prices as weights, and the like. It also permits observation of distinct patterns of change over time that allow for differences in interrelations between the short and the long run, rather than having all change lumped into a single complex qualified only by stochastic disturbances. The degree of formality of the models used in interpretation of limited stretches of economic experi-

28

ence, particularly new stretches or newly measured ones, is set by the balancing of gains from a formal set of parameters against losses. The losses are not slight if the formal model conceals revealing deviations by impounding them in anonymous variance, or if modifying any part of the model involves long scrutiny and heavy costs. When the changing economic reality is teaching us something new at a rapid rate, the costs of formalizing prior limited knowledge by dint of a variety of assumptions (substitutes for knowledge that is lacking) may be too heavy, and the gain from having results amenable to formal tests of uncertain relevance may be too slight.

3. RECENT TRENDS IN QUANTITATIVE ECONOMIC RESEARCH

Quantitative economic research on the broader aspects of the national economy, dealing with the growth and structure of national product, its origin and distribution, is dependent upon a supply of primary data sufficient for a variety of meaningful economic measures. These, combined with complementary data and relevant hypotheses, can then be interpreted and eventually serve as a foundation for at least partial generalizations and tentative predictions. In turning to trends in quantitative research of this broad type since World War II in this country, I must limit the discussion to studies that employ national product and related aggregates, largely for the analysis of short- and long-term changes in the performance of national economies. This performance is viewed in relation to the commonly accepted goals, e.g., adequate growth, freedom from disturbing fluctuations, equitable distribution of gains, the least painful distribution of losses, and the like. Much of what can be said of this type of quantitative research on the broader aggregates for national economies (and their major components) applies equally to quantitative research dealing with some important economic institutions that are part of the framework of national economies, or with activities of the major policy agencies, or with the special problems imposed by international relations (rather than viewing the "rest of the world" as a minor sector in the national product total). But since my knowledge of these other areas is slight, I shall limit my review to the field with which I am more, if not fully, familiar—a field to which the National Bureau has contributed much in the past, and the prospects and problems of which must be considered in any discussion of the National Bureau's programs for the future.

Acceleration in the Supply of Primary Data, Economic Measures, and the Pace of Quantitative Research

A look back over the period since the middle 1940's, and comparing it with the interwar period, conveys a strong impression of an acceleration in the supply of primary data, of economic measures, and of the pace of quantitative research related to the national economy, in this country and elsewhere. Output of primary data is not easily measured, because reduction to comparable units is feasible only for the most elementary types of information (e.g., the number of people counted). This is also true of the generation of economic measures, which, as already indicated, may be complex amalgams of primary data with economic concepts and theories, and with wide quality and significance differentials. As

30

to pace of quantitative research, some measure of input and gross output can be secured, if quality differentials are disregarded; but the effort may not be worthwhile, and in any case is not feasible here. I am thus limited to impressions, supported by some evidence.

Let me begin with the most telling set of economic measures, that of national product, its components, and the related totals, for this country. The initial study by the National Bureau in the early 1920's made a significant contribution in attempting to provide some answers to the major question of the day, the distribution of income; and this contribution marked a substantial advance over the earlier work of several individual scholars. The notable expansion of the National Bureau's work and indeed of any work in this field in this country did not come until the 1930's. It was largely in response to the acute need to take stock of an economy afflicted by a major depression and to a changing emphasis on the problems of investment and savings generated by the writings of John Maynard Keynes.

But the major acceleration in the supply of *continuous* estimates of national product, in increasing detail and with an increasingly solid foundation in a variety of primary data, began when estimation was taken over by the Department of Commerce; and when, soon after World War II, the results became a frequently used guide to public and much of private policy. This acceleration was stimulated by the increasing contribution of economic scholarship outside the government, which generated the flow-of-funds approach, the input-output analysis, new devices for sampling and summarization, and a host of other intellectual innovations that served to facilitate and to stimulate an ever-increasing flow of economic measures,

31

produced in rising proportions by the government agencies. To be sure, this type of acceleration can hardly be measured by percentage rates of increase: after all, when one starts with nothing or very little, the initial proportional increase can be enormous and cannot be exceeded later. Nor does any government initiate economic measures that have not already been explored, and their worth demonstrated, by individual scholars or research agencies that are the main carriers of innovative research. The acceleration of which I speak was an enormous increase in the volume of acceptable economic measures, in increasing detail for any given time and in growing coverage of the historical experience. In this case, the possible economies of scale, in terms of facilitating significant economic research, are so great that linear measures of quantities and proportions are hardly appropriate. Since national product estimates are closely linked with other economic measures that may have an independent value for other uses (price indexes, money supply, labor force and employment, and the like), acceleration in the supply of measures relating to national product and its significant components must have meant acceleration in the supply of other economic measures as well.

What was true of the United States, when one compares the post-World War II situation with that of the interwar period, appears to have been true of other countries that we now classify as economically developed. The assumption of official responsibility for continuous, detailed, and acceptable estimation of national product and its components has been largely a World War II or post-World War II phenomenon in most developed countries of the world.[4] The extension of official income estimation was even more striking for the less developed countries of the world. Many of them attained political independence only after World War II, and their governments then faced the problems of assuring adequate levels of performance and growth of the economy, in the concern for which even approximate estimates of aggregate product and its major components seemed indispensable. The explosive expansion in the supply of national product measures the world over in the post-World War II years can be seen by comparing the summaries of these estimates by the United Nations in the late 1940's or early 1950's with what is available in the massive *Yearbook of National Accounts Statistics* for recent years; or by comparing the latter with the League of Nations publications in the 1930's. A similar explosive increase occurred in the supply of data on the balance of international payments in the international compendia of the IMF; on population in the *Demographic Yearbook* of the United Nations; on labor force in the publications of the ILO; on agriculture in those of the FAO; and on education and health in the yearbooks of other UN agencies. Even the Communist countries, after a temporary blackout, began to release more meaningful economic measures after World War II. Communist China and a few of its satellites are significant exceptions. There, if an increased supply is produced

[4] Previously an occasional elaborate estimate had been prepared, but without a continuous follow-up. See Paul Studenski, *The Income of Nations,* New York, New York University Press, 1958, the first 150 pages of which cover the developments before World War I; see also the United Nations, Statistical Office, *National Income Statistics, 1938–47,* New York, 1948, and *National Income Statistics, 1938–1948,* New York, 1950.

by and available to the government, it is withheld from circulation. The exception is of some significance to the relation between supply of economic measures produced under governmental auspices and quantitative research.

If we accept the impression of a marked acceleration after World War II in the supply of national product estimates and of a wide variety of related economic measures, occurring both in this country and in many other countries, two questions arise.

First, does this also mean an acceleration in the supply of primary data—over and beyond the usual accretion associated with continuation of the old patterns of census-taking, periodic reporting, etc.; or does it mean merely more intensive reworking of the stock of primary data growing at the rate prevailing in the earlier years? In a sense it does not matter which answer is valid. Primary data existed before, but may not have been utilized as raw material for meaningful economic measures. This situation was not untypical of the nineteenth and early twentieth centuries, when data were being published in census volumes and statistical compendia but only gathered dust. During that period quantitative-research-oriented economists (or governments) made little attempt to convert the data into meaningful economic measures, thereby testing their quality and relevance to economic analysis. Until they are so tested, the unused primary data have little value for economic research and analysis. In that sense the initial utilization of existing primary data for formulation of acceptable economic measures (such as estimates of national product and its significant components) is like the supply of new primary data. It provides a base for economic analysis and quantitative research not previously available.

34

Yet, there must also have been an acceleration in the supply of basic primary data: some in response to pressures generated by the accelerated attempts to provide meaningful economic measures, and others associated with the factors that explain the more rapid pace of quantitative economic research. If greater attempts were made to combine primary data with other information, and to convert them into economic measures acceptable in terms of the underlying basic assumptions and theoretical hypotheses, and if in this process the available primary data proved deficient, such attempts acted as a stimulus to supplement the existing primary data. In that sense, work on a comprehensive and articulated estimate like that of national incomes provides an incentive for, and a guide to, the collection of missing primary data—especially if they are crucial. Furthermore, if the technology of collecting and processing primary data improves markedly, as it did in recent decades, the resulting reduction in the real costs of deriving the indispensable summaries may, all other conditions being equal, permit a corresponding acceleration in the collection and tabulation of new primary data. The acceleration in the supply of such comprehensive and basic economic measures as national product and its components must have also meant an acceleration in the flow of primary data—even in some developed countries like the United States and the Scandinavian countries where periodic collection of various basic nationwide statistics has been a practice since the late eighteenth and early nineteenth centuries. There is little doubt about the acceleration in the flow of primary data after World War II in the less developed countries and in many of those developed nations that

35

were not distinguished by adequate data collection in the pre-World War II days.

The second question, whether the pace of quantitative economic research and perhaps of all economic research also accelerated, is, despite some fuzziness in the definition of a rate of output of economic research, at least answerable in terms of inputs. If the supply of primary data and that of economic measures accelerated, one could certainly argue that the pace of economic research was also accelerating. And, unless the total volume of economic research ceased to grow, or unless the increasing supply of measures and primary data had a *diminishing* effect on "quantization" of economic analysis, one would expect an acceleration in the pace of *quantitative* economic research. Moreover, one would expect that in free market economies, in addition to individual scholars, organized research institutes, and governmental and quasi-governmental agencies, at least the larger business units and trade unions would undertake systematic, quantitative research.

Some evidence is at hand concerning inputs into research. Although a thorough assembly and analysis of such information is beyond the limits of this paper, I can cite some figures available for this country. The number of doctoral degrees in economics (including agricultural economics) granted by American universities rose from 117 per year for the decade from the mid-1920's to the mid-1930's to 132 per year in the next decade; it then jumped to 250 per year in the six years from 1946 through 1951, to 313 in 1957, and was as high as 680 in 1967.[5] While a rising proportion of Ph.D. degrees in

[5] For the earlier years see Howard G. Bowen, "Graduate Education in Economics," *American Economic Review,* vol. XLIII, no. 4, part

economics may have been awarded to foreign students, the acceleration shown above would hardly be reduced significantly by a reasonable adjustment for this factor. The United States members of the American Economic Association (excluding subscribers), estimated to be less than 2.5 thousand in 1920–1924, rose to about 4 thousand by 1944–1946, and reached 15.6 thousand in 1969.[6] The impression is that the number of people actively interested in economics, particularly those highly qualified for the pursuit of economic research, has grown at an accelerated rate since World War II, and presumably made possible a higher pace of economic research, including quantitative. (The above statement disregards the higher level of training of the more recent products of graduate education.) A similar impression of acceleration after the late 1930's, and particularly after World War II, is produced by the marked expansion in the size of the older professional journals, and by the addition of a number of new ones.

But it would hardly be useful to try to document further these rather strong impressions of acceleration in the supply of data, of economic measures, and in the pace of quantitative economic research. The illustrations and comments above should suffice to yield a conclusion most relevant to any consideration of the National Bureau's program for the future. In the early 1920's, and perhaps through the first fifteen to twenty years of its

2, September 1953, Table 41, pp. 209–10; for the later years see the Behavioral and Social Sciences Survey Committee, *The Behavioral and Social Sciences: Outlook and Needs,* Englewood Cliffs, N.J., 1969, Table 9-5, p. 146.

[6] See the *American Economic Review, 1969 Handbook of the American Economic Association,* vol. LIX, no. 6, January 1970, Table 2, pp. 593–594, and Table 4, p. 596.

existence, the National Bureau was one of the few loci of quantitative economic research in this country. However, while remaining a major center for quantitative economic research, in recent decades it has become a much smaller part, proportionately, of the total resources devoted to such research, particularly when one includes, as one should, research done by government agencies. Incidentally, the number of books published by the National Bureau also indicates a rapid acceleration (see NBER, *Publications 1920–1970,* March 1970). Publications in the general and special series grew from 66 for 1921–1945 to 115 for 1946–1969; with conference volumes and occasional and technical papers included, the number of titles is 102 for the earlier period, and 279 for the later. Even so, the rapid expansion in the volume of quantitative economic research, and the resources invested in it in the country at large, calls for a careful scrutiny of the particular contribution that the National Bureau is best prepared to make.

Causes of Acceleration

Of more interest than detailed evidence on the post-World War II acceleration in the supply of primary data and economic measures, and the pace of quantitative economic research, are the factors that might explain such an acceleration. The explanation, tentative as it must be, should tell us much about the relation of economic research to the major problems that it is meant to resolve; help us to identify the problems that still urgently demand, if not solutions (which may be out of reach), at least the amelioration that economic research and policy may provide; and permit us to project the

38

possible problems and tasks of research for the future.

Since supply of primary data, production of economic measures, and the pace of quantitative economic research are interrelated, an explanation of the acceleration in one of these complexes explains to a large extent the acceleration in the others. Likewise, the initiative taken by one social agency, e.g., the government, in intensifying the flow of data, measures, and perhaps the pace of research, stimulates a higher pace of research among other agencies, such as academic economists, nongovernmental research institutions, and business firms or trade unions. Yet it is next to impossible to treat these interrelated complexes as one. At the risk of drawing artificial distinctions, we will discuss (i) the assumption of wider responsibility by government for growth, stability, and equity in the national economy, and consider what seem to us the major factors that brought about this increased responsibility, particularly in the older, free market, developed economies. Since these factors also stimulate scholarly work, we consider (ii) how the response of scholarly research to emerging problems interplays with the change in the scope of government responsibility. We then conclude (iii) by considering the changes in tools, analytical and mechanical, that, by increasing the efficiency of inputs, may have contributed to the acceleration in the pace of output of economic research.

(i) The governments of a large proportion of the countries of the world, unweighted or weighted by population or product, had, by the late 1960's, professed to assume responsibility for greater economic growth, full and stable employment, greater equity, and the like. That

39

proportion is larger than in the mid-1940's; and larger by far than in the early 1920's, when only the newly organized and struggling USSR could be so classified. This does not mean that governments were not always interested in facilitating such goals. But it was generally assumed in the free market economies that, given a minimal framework of political, legal, and social stability, greater economic growth, stability, and equity could be achieved without, rather than with, active government intervention. Moreover, there was doubt that, if government did assume direct overt responsibility for such broad aspects of economic performance, it would know what action to take to discharge such a responsibility.

One thus gets the impression that in the past only narrowly defined economic problems were directly tackled and acted upon by government. Some of these dealt with monopolies and trusts, the deficiencies of the banking and credit institutions in preventing economic crises, the effects of tariffs on specific domestic industries, labor, and immigration (I am citing examples from the United States experience). These were problems created by inadequacies in the prevailing market institutions; and a great deal of economic research was generated by government when each problem was studied. But there was no strong conviction that the broader aspects of growth, stability, and equity should be a continuous and active concern of the government; there was no pressure, like that exerted today, to observe continuously the rate of growth, level of employment, degree of price and other stability, of the economy at large. Nor was there a widely shared belief (recognized in official legislation) that government has an active responsibility for these broader aspects of the national economy. It is,

40

of course, this shift toward greater government responsibility that resulted in the acceleration of the supply of primary data, economic measures, and the pace of economic research—insofar as government initiative, resources, and pressures were responsible.

What caused this shift? The answer to this question for Communist countries is automatic, since widespread control of the economy by the government, in turn dominated by a single political party, is of the essence—with all the familiar consequences for other economic and social institutions. The answer to the question for the many less developed countries that have only recently acquired political independence may lie in the fact that the personnel who are staffing the new governments are those few with some economic training; and these governments must play a crucial role in the economic and social modernization required to accelerate economic growth. It is for the older, developed, free market economies that the question assumes most interest. In these countries the rate of growth was more satisfactory; occasional instabilities were cushioned by a higher standard of living; and, despite inequalities, inequities were of far narrower proportions than elsewhere. What factors then exercised pressure toward assumption of wider responsibility by the government for these broader aspects of economic performance, rather than, as in the past, leaving them to the working of the market and other private economic and social institutions?

No definitive answer can be given to the question, if only because the consequence to be explained—the shift in overtly accepted responsibility by governments—is itself not precisely defined. It can range from purely political and empty eloquence to a far-reaching positive action by the government, involving a volume of re-sources that is large in relation to the rest of the economy. But if we assume that the shift in question has real substance, a number of related factors seem to provide an impetus to and an explanation of it.

Some of these factors lie in the demonstrated failure of the economic system, as it operated heretofore in these free market developed countries under conditions that were not so exceptional as to warrant the failure. The impact of the great depression of the 1930's was particularly far-reaching. If, with all the adjustments that had previously been made in many developed economies, particularly financial and monetary controls, the contraction in the capacity of these economies to exploit fully their resources could be so disastrous, the existing institutional controls were inadequate and needed to be modified. The modification might have been limited to new provisions for unemployment insurance, new plans for supplementary public works, and the like, if it were not for the Keynesian theory—partly generated by the pressure of events on scholarly analysis. This theory indicated that such a situation could recur if government did not take care to assure adequacy of final demand at a sufficiently high level. And once government had to assume an active role in supplementing private investment opportunities, questions of economic growth and the implicitly greater responsibility of government for such growth—if only in terms of its role in complementing private demand and private investment opportunities—were bound to arise. One should also note that the connection between major depressions and economic growth problems became all the more evident when the distortion of the political and economic structure in Hitler's Germany (and the growth

42

consequences that followed) was seen as having been made possible, in large part, by the disaffection of the population as a result of the prolonged depression.

The other factor was World War II and its aftermath. Active participation by a country in a major war is clearly an exceptional set of conditions under which the "normal" operation of market and other economic and social institutions must be drastically modified—the more so, the greater the magnitude of the conflict. The main reason, of course, is that a large volume of resources must be devoted to the ultimate social gain of avoiding defeat, and no clear connection with measurable private gain is apparent. The sovereign government must assume responsibility for mobilizing such resources, since it alone can exercise the political and legal authority— backed by social consensus—to limit activities oriented toward private gain, and free the resources required for the socially necessary war task. It is plausible to argue that the experience during a prolonged major war, the successful redirection by the government of economic activity toward a new set of purposes, makes for easier acceptance even in relatively peaceful times of a more active role of government with respect to economic growth, stability, and equity. The effect is stronger if the postwar years are characterized by international divisiveness, with a continuing active international competition in terms of precisely these broader economic aspects. The cold war has certainly contributed to the consensus in favor of greater responsibility of central government for many tasks in which the national economy plays a basic role; and in which national security and national position in the international competition had to be considered together with domestic aspects of economic performance—the adequacy of which, in itself, assumed significance for the country's international position.

The divided state of the post-World War II world, with the major Communist country, the USSR, viewing itself as beleaguered by a hostile capitalist ring and using all its power to widen the base under its control, constituted both a threat and a challenge to the free market developed countries. It was a threat in that the revolution in the manufacture and transportation of armaments reduced markedly the protection that distance had offered previously. As a result, a warlike situation tended to be maintained, with a large volume of resources devoted by the central government to security-oriented economic production. The challenge lay in the claim of Communist countries that their's was a more effective way to attain a higher rate of economic growth, a greater degree of stability, and even wider equity. The validity of such claims had to be examined, and the overt and hidden costs appraised. But an even more important response to the challenge lay in a re-examination of the rate and conditions of economic growth in the free market economies themselves; and in a scrutiny of the capacity of the older institutions to operate under the changed conditions of the new and divided world. For example, would validity still attach to the theory held by the established institutions, that the promotion of competition would result in success for the more able and productive members in the race, if there was an ever-present threat of being called away from this competition into national defense, or of being destroyed in an atomic holocaust before the competition was completed? Much of the shift toward a welfare state in the older established and developed free market economies was the result of a natural

44

trend from legal to political, and from political to economic equality. However, much of the shift in the post-World War II years was also the result of a recognition that economic inequalities were no longer justifiable on the grounds of their presumptive contribution to productivity in the market-oriented part of the system, in view of the increasing weight of the required contribution to other high-priority social purposes, with respect to which certain aspects of economic inequality are destructive, not constructive. Just as it proved important to control capital investment and channel savings, without leaving the decision entirely to the private sector of the economy, so it became necessary to be concerned with inequalities in personal income generated by the competitive characteristics of private enterprise. And the underlying international, intersystem competition and challenge had obvious effects on the relations between the developed market economies and the less developed countries, many of which were former colonies. The evolution of new forms of international transfer of resources from the rich developed to the poor less developed countries also meant a new type of activity and responsibility for the government, because of the inadequacy of the ordinary channels of private enterprise.

If the Great Depression, the ensuing war, and the post-World War II intersystem competition in the world were among the more obvious factors responsible for the shift in the free market developed economies toward greater responsibility by the governments for economic growth, stability, and equity, two other groups of factors, less conspicuous and noticeable, may also have contributed. One was connected with the rapid development of technology, the major permissive source of mod-

45

ern economic growth, to levels at which innovations could have highly potent and dangerous implications. The marked advances in mechanical power at the disposal of human beings, in rapidity of penetration into the various areas on this planet, and recently beyond it, resulted in diseconomies of mass output under private enterprise that called for remedies possible only with intervention of public authority. Moreover, and even more important, these advances created opportunities for innovations with so much power, and hence so great a danger of misuse, that it was unsafe to leave them in the hands of private enterprise, even if the latter were capable and willing to take the economic risks involved. Thus the technological innovation, war-originated, that resulted in a designed production of atomic energy, carried with it such great danger that careful government decisions were required on how its mass exploitation could be safely developed by private enterprise. Space exploration, another essentially war-originated innovation, involved such a huge volume of inputs and was so far removed from market exploitation that only the government could undertake it—although some of its by-products are already exploitable for private market purposes. The problem that would arise if and when the present work on DNA makes it possible to control the genetic capacities of future generations is another good illustration of a technological innovation that would require control by a socially responsible government. One might, in general, argue that any major technological and scientific innovation, which has dangerous by-products or bestows too much power on its users, cannot be entrusted to private enterprise without careful supervision,

46

and must be controlled by the government until these dangers can be observed and counteracted.

The second additional complex of factors that might have contributed to assumption by governments of a more active concern with the broader aspects of economic performance is the progress made in the very course of study of the new conditions and the new data, which resulted in revisions of the older theories that implicitly limited government responsibility to keeping order and dealing with immediate emergencies. To illustrate: if the main source of economic growth is assumed to be material capital, and hence savings, and government can only encourage such savings and their efficient utilization, its responsibility is limited to the institutional changes that serve this means of optimizing economic growth. However, if the major source of economic growth is technological change, and if the latter can be facilitated by research, particularly the type that, while basic and immensely productive in the long run, yields results that cannot be appropriated by private interests, then the government must undertake the task, or finance it. To illustrate further: the long-term growth rate can differ widely among free market economies, as it has in fact done during the postwar decades. If these differences reflect a variety of policies pursued by governments, i.e., if the process of economic growth, income distribution, and temporal stability, are not subject to some inexorable laws over which intervention by government can have no useful influence—there is no reason to *limit in advance* the concern of government with the broader aspects of economic activity.

What is most relevant in this connection is that, while the progress of tested study of observable growth be-

47

havior of even free market economies tends to remove limits on the possible contribution of government, it also tends to weaken any theories that claim inexorable laws of behavior for private enterprise or the indubitable virtue of some ideological forms of social and economic organization. And this abandonment of dogmatic notions leads both to an acceleration of quantitative research (and of other types of research) and to the pragmatic initiative by governments in assuming responsibility for the basic performance of the economy. It is hardly an accident that Adam Smith was scornful of what political arithmetic could teach him, not so much because its empirical standards were so low but because he firmly believed that the truth of what he thought made for the wealth of nations needed no empirical support. To be sure, his thesis, with its implications, was based in part on the historical experience of Western European societies as he saw them; and he was quite sensitive to the realistic conditions that might limit the full application of the principle to specific problems. But the impression remains that it was only with Malthus, whose thesis was applied to sources of poverty (rather than of wealth), that the search for preventive checks and a more consistent interest in observational data began. It is no accident that, in Communist countries, the dogmatic conviction concerning the rightness of a special type of control and organization of the economy is accompanied not merely by neglect of various aspects of quantitative economic analysis but also by direct prohibition of the wide range of quantitative economic study pursued in societies less committed in this fashion. The variety of growth experience revealed by further study in the United States and other developed countries, and the abandonment of sim-

48

plistic and dogmatic notions concerning causes of economic progress and related requirements as to income distribution, or tolerance of income instabilities, contributed to the more pragmatic, and hence potentially wider, concern of governments with economic growth, stability, and equity.

(ii) The problems and challenges posed by domestic and international history that induced governments of free market economies to assume wider responsibility for the economy were naturally a stimulus also to economists and research institutions outside of government. If the more intensive analysis of new data and measures established a more pragmatic view, one less constrained by dogmatic notions of what government activity could contribute, it was clearly the type of research pursued by nongovernment agencies that could have this effect of weakening old theoretical notions and viewpoints. In general, and because it is too closely involved with current problems, economic research under government auspices is likely to be conservative, following established definitions and measures and applying them to current problems, often accepting without question the bases of the measures themselves. Few economic measures have been adopted by government agencies in the older free market societies until they had been advanced and experimented with in the scholarly literature. The experience in this country with estimates of national income and product, input-output approaches, flow-of-funds measures, and even periodic sample surveys, clearly illustrates the sequence from academic and research institute scholarship to government use.

But the stimulus to quantitative economic research

49

provided by the expanded responsibility and activities of the governments is only part of the story. I have the impression that, in this country (and perhaps elsewhere), the acceleration in quantitative economic research was not only the result of government expansion, either directly or through the granting of funds. After all, major economic problems that called for more economic research, quantitative research included, have always existed, but they have not apparently produced the acceleration in the pace of economic research suggested by the increase in numbers of potential scholars in this country, cited above.

In fact, the acceleration in the numbers of trained economists was part of a much wider movement, affecting all levels of advanced study in a wide variety of disciplines. Limiting ourselves to the numbers of Ph.D. degrees awarded, as a rough indication of the new potential research scholars, we find that the *total* accelerated at a more rapid rate than the number of economists —the latter forming but a small fraction, ranging from about 3.5 to about 6 per cent of the total. The average share of Ph.D. degrees in economics in the total (arithmetic means of annual shares) was 5.8 per cent in the decade from the mid-1920's to the mid-1930's; 4.8 per cent in the following decade; back to 5.7 per cent in the six years from 1946 through 1951 (the period when the great acceleration in numbers began); dropped to 3.6 per cent in 1957; and was only 3.4 per cent in 1967 (see the sources cited above). Furthermore, from 1957 to 1967, the share of economics Ph.D.'s in the total for all behavioral and social sciences declined from 18.8 to 17.4 per cent; and political science, psychology and educational psychology, and sociology (including rural so-
50

ciology) showed a greater rise than economics (the latter including agricultural economics).[7] This suggests that the acceleration in numbers of trained potential contributors to economic research was part of a wider movement, and cannot be attributed to the nature of the new economic problems or to the greater responsibility of government for the broader aspects of the economy.

The causes of this wider expansion in higher education, particularly in its most advanced stages, would form a fascinating topic for investigation. Offhand, one would expect to see it as a response to the much higher valuation placed on its contribution to society and to the individual—a reflection of the connection between the recent technological innovations and advanced stages of scientific and experimental knowledge, and the more advanced methods of social and behavioral sciences, as applied to policy problems within both the public and private sectors. This connection would be reflected in the higher compensation to individuals with advanced knowledge in the arts and sciences, as well as in the extensive financial help to graduate students and other advanced learners. Economic inducements at the undergraduate level of education must also have been greater,

[7] See the sources cited in footnotes 5 and 6. With the annual number of Ph.D.'s in economics increasing from 132 in the decade from 1934–35 to 1944–45 to 680 in 1967 and the growth in the total number of Ph.D.'s even greater, the contribution of the larger numbers of the relevant age groups must have been quite small. The most relevant group, men age 25–34, increased from 1940 to 1970 by less than 20 per cent, much less than the total population because of the low birth rates in the late 1930's and early 1940's. For the underlying data see *Historical Statistics of the United States,* Washington, D.C., 1960; *Continuation to 1962,* Washington, D.C., 1965; and *Statistical Abstract of the United States, 1971,* Washington, D.C., 1971.

to widen appreciably the base from which the movement into more advanced training was possible. Such wider inducements were probably provided by differential returns in connection with years of education and by lower real costs associated with a higher level of per capita product and income for an increasing proportion of the population. One could also argue that, given the high-income propensity of demand for education as a consumption good, higher per capita income alone, without the favorable economic differentials associated with years of education, would have brought about an acceleration of secondary and higher education in the post-World War II period, after the backlog of the depressed 1930's and the restrictive conditions of World War II. One could also argue that the demand for education as a *consumption* good was particularly high in recent decades, when better understanding of the events in those years of rapid change placed high value on education—not as a means of earning extra income but as a means of orienting oneself in a difficult world. If such orientation required the equivalent of a good college education, the latter incidentally provided a rapidly widening base for the more advanced types of training and preparation for research, reducing in a sense the cost of information needed for such choices.

Adequate analysis of the acceleration of advanced education in almost all disciplines, of its effect on the pace of research productive of current and future innovations, and of the several reasons for it, would involve comparative study of a number of developed economies that have institutions permitting effective free choice by individuals. Such a study is beyond the limits of this paper and of my capacities. But it is useful to note here

52

that the quickening in the growth of numbers of new potential contributors to economic research, including the quantitative, is part of a broader movement, not limited to the effects of a shift toward greater government responsibility even in the free market economies. The implications for our topic are twofold.

First, regardless of the possible continuation of such acceleration, the proximate future may be affected by the innovational changes that the larger body of research scholars is likely to generate. And the rate at which it generates such innovations may rise, even if the marginal contribution of the larger body is lower than that of a smaller body (although it need not be, in a relatively inexhaustible field), so long as the decline in marginal efficiency is more than compensated for by the larger numbers and possible economies of scale. Thus, as we look ahead to the problems of economic research, we ought to be thinking in terms of a *greater* rate of scientific and technological innovation—rather than assume that the high rate of the immediate past represents a kind of plateau or is transitory.

The second implication is more closely related to the possible immediate prospects for economic research. If the numbers of new, highly trained, potential research scholars accelerated more rapidly in related social science and behavioral disciplines than in economics, the research *output* of these disciplines may also have accelerated. Since this output is closely related to the economic, particularly in the analysis of long-term problems of growth and structure, it would presumably have validity and relevance for economic research proper. Indeed, the increasing concern of quantitative economic studies with demographic aspects of economic growth, with the

53

effects of political structure, with discrimination and stratification, clearly indicates that the nature of the problems is breaking down the traditionally narrow discipline boundaries. One, therefore, must consider the possibility that the output of research, quantitative and other, in the related social sciences and behavioral disciplines has accelerated substantially, and that its more effective utilization may be an important prerequisite in any considered plans and prospective programs for economic research.

(iii) There is little question that, over the twenty-five years since World War II, tremendous strides have been made in the methods of collecting and summarizing primary data, and subjecting it to elaborate computations and manipulations of increasing complexity. Strides have also been made in developing rules of inference from quantitative data, and in building models, simple or complex, that simulate what appear to be the most relevant structural and behavior characteristics of the national economies or of significant sectors within them, thus providing more formal and more discriminating alternatives for organizing and interpreting a vast variety of economic measures. Given, in addition, the acceleration in the numbers of potential research economists with increasingly advanced training, we could assume an increased pace of quantitative economic research. Indeed, we might even interpret it as an acceleration in the *output* of economic research, if we could assume that, over the last two decades and a half, neither the rise in efficiency nor the complexity of the analytical problems with reference to which we can judge the "finishedness" of the output of quantitative economic research had changed from what it had been in the past.

54

The above statement refers to three, quite distinct, possible sources of rise in efficiency of research inputs. The first is the material technology for collecting and handling primary data and for any derivative measures. Considering the major technological changes after World War II in the field of communication, calculation, and reproduction of information (some based on war-induced types of innovation), one may conclude that the contribution from this source to efficiency of inputs in quantitative research grew at a distinctly higher rate in recent than in the pre-World War II decades.

The second source is represented by the rapid advances that have been made in the theory of inferences from quantitative data. The latter are now being viewed (as they are in much of statistical theory) as reflections of a formally structured universe that can be reduced by analysis to a mixture of invariant and variant components. Distinctions are thus made between approximations to central tendencies and normal variance, or the different structure of small sample variances, or the application of mathematical tools to cyclical and trend components and the like, or the application of other mathematical tools of particular promise to specific economic behavior patterns that lend themselves to meaningful constraints. The resulting tools—some statistical, some econometric, some elements in formal economic theory—can hardly be reduced to comparable units for measuring the additions over the last twenty-five years against those in the preceding decades; and my knowledge of the field is far too limited to permit tenable judgments. Yet I have the impression, supported by chronology of advance in the theory of sampling, design, and statistical inference, the emergence and flowering of econometrics as a subdiscipline, and developments in

55

mathematical economics, that there is an acceleration in the rate at which the stock of these tools has grown. It seems to me that this stock has proved, after sufficient testing, to have substantially increased the efficiency of post-World War II quantitative economic research.

The third possible source of greater efficiency is the formulation and multiplication of substantive, theoretical hypotheses, relevant to observable reality, which perforce stimulate closely associated economic research. Keynesian general theory was neither an innovation in material technology of data collection or computation, nor did it constitute an advance in the methodology of statistical inference, or in econometrics, or the applied mathematical tools of the corresponding division of economic theory. Yet it proved to be a great stimulus to quantitative economic research, primarily through the emphasis that it placed on savings and capital investment, and on the factors that determined these two components of total product (viewed at the use level) and of total income (viewed at the allocation level). This statement is true also of other hypotheses and models that have emerged in discussions concerning major factors in aggregate growth—at least when these hypotheses or models specify the factors sufficiently to permit establishing their quantitative counterparts, and are not destroyed at the outset by what little is already known of certain quantitative aspects of the economic growth of nations. All such hypotheses and theories are attempts at new generalizations, either cancelling or adding to those already available; and their implications, either for broad judgments of the course of economic affairs or for more specific policy, are sufficiently intriguing to warrant quantitative analysis. A greater supply can potentially raise the efficiency of quantitative economic research by providing stimuli and guidance, and thus hold promise of more meaningful results.

We cannot state firmly that the flow of hypotheses and theories relevant to quantitative economic research dealing with broader aspects of national economies was more rapid during the post-World War II years than previously. However, we do feel that the rate of addition of such hypotheses as could serve to guide quantitative research, because they were formulated in a more easily testable way, was higher than in the past, when our knowledge of the quantitative outlines of national economies was so limited. And it may well be that the same impression would be conveyed if we were to look at many major aspects of economic analysis. If the pace was greater for theorizing about the performance of the national economy, it would have its ramifications in affecting such major aspects as industrial organization, supply of natural resources, fiscal and monetary policy and theory, and international trade and capital movements.

All of this may mean a greater pace of *intermediate* output of economic research, of economic measures, partial and partially tested hypotheses, interpretations of new stretches of economic experience, and revised interpretations of some old stretches. But what this means for the pace of *finished* output of economic research, i.e., generalizations tested and established within conditions that assure sufficient relevance in application to *realistic* prediction, either for better understanding of what is likely to occur or for better evaluation of the effects of policy, depends on one's judgments of relevance and realism. These would vary with the nature and scope of

57

the economic process or structure that forms the focus of such a generalization. Thus, the generalization concerning the cyclical responsiveness of graduated personal income taxes in developed free market economies with established income tax traditions, and on the assumption of realistic conditions concerning income changes, price changes, and the like, can probably be put into a relatively finished form—given the supply of primary data, the econometric tools for analysis, and the battery of hypotheses concerning cyclical sensitivity of various types of income and the relation of the latter to income level. (This may be too optimistic a judgment, but let me use it as an illustration.) On the other hand, it is difficult to think of any tested generalization, significantly specific to permit the quantitative prediction of aggregate growth, or even of changes in the structural parameters in the course of growth (of, let us say, the free market economy) that may be viewed as even approximating a "finished" product—notwithstanding the multitude of such tentative generalizations, cross-section studies, and econometric exercises. At any rate, here we are in the area of difficult judgments, which should perhaps be advanced only with elaborate documentation, not feasible in this paper. If suffices to point out, in concluding our discussion of the acceleration in the pace of quantitative economic research, that, in addition to the changed position of governments (particularly in the developed free market economies) and acceleration in the supply of highly trained potential economic research scholars, there was also a quickening of the pace of improvement in the material technology of collection and handling of quantitative data, in the methodological tools for analysis of a wide variety of complex types of measurement, and

58

possibly also in the flow of theories, sufficiently well formulated to guide quantitative economic research in more "productive" directions.

4. IDENTIFYING MAJOR RESEARCH PROBLEMS

Persistence of Unsolved Problems

The greater supply of data and economic measures and the accelerated flow of hypotheses and pace of research do not mean that we are now in the happy situation of having answered all major questions and provided an adequate basis for realistic prediction and optimal economic policy. It only means that we have learned a great deal, enough perhaps to force abandonment of earlier simpler and more restrictive theories and to replace them with new hypotheses, more relevant but still based upon many simplifying and restrictive assumptions. It means that there is a basis for a greater consensus on the major changes that occurred in the economy and perhaps on some of the major factors that contributed to these changes. And it means that the greater supply of tested data and of realistic partial hypotheses permits a better evaluation of the implications of the changes as a guide to action. It also means a better choice of policy priorities and perhaps of specific policies—insofar as better knowledge of the basic framework and changes in the economy, and more tested analysis of policies, can affect both the overall priorities and specific policy choices. But acceleration in the supply of data and in the pace of research brings forth a variety of unsolved major problems calling for further

59

research and analysis. These problems may be in the form of puzzles generated by conflict between the new findings and the old theories; or they may emerge as aspects of recent economic change, whose major determining factors cannot yet be reliably identified; or they may be associated with socially undesirable consequences, for proper judgment of which neither current measurement nor quantitative analysis has yet provided a basis.

Indeed, the pattern of jubilee-occasioned discussion illustrated by this paper—and by some of the other colloquia organized within the past year by the National Bureau—is first to review the recent course of research and make laudatory remarks about the accomplishment; and then to observe the problems still to be properly resolved, which are almost overwhelming in their complexity and recalcitrance. This may be a reflection of the occupational bias of research workers, who naturally tend to weight new unsolved problems more heavily than the older, more familiar, and at least partly resolved, problems. But without attempting to gauge magnitudes and compare present inventories of unsolved questions with those of twenty-five or fifty years ago, we cannot deny that this sequence of much research, much learning, and much still to be resolved is a realistic description of all experimental and observational intellectual disciplines. It is often referred to as the "endless frontier" of science, a term to designate the inexhaustible supply of significant problems for further research.[8] I see no

[8] This statement may now be challenged for some divisions of basic natural science, according to Bentley Glass in his presidential address to the American Association for the Advancement of Science (see his "Science: Endless Horizons or Golden Age," *Science*, vol. 171, no. 3966, 8/1/1971, pp. 23–29).

reason to deviate from this pattern in reference to quantitative economic research on growth, stability, and equity in the economies of this country and others. But before trying to identify the major problems and their priorities in further research, it may be well to consider why such unsolved problems emerge after decades of accelerated research, particularly in economics in which (as well as in other social sciences) the situation may differ significantly from that in the natural sciences.

The reference to "endless frontier" suggests that, as data and measures improve and tested generalization and theory succeed in identifying general and invariant properties, the new insights and the better tools reveal previously unseen aspects of the universe at its largest, and of the basic characteristics of matter at its smallest. But even in experimental sciences, let alone observational natural sciences, additional data and better tools are provided not only in response to questions generated by the inner logic of existing theories. Even then, questions posed by the old theories may, when pursued, yield answers that indicate the need for major revisions of the theories and thus generate a host of new research problems. But in many cases the new data and tools are provided because of events exogenous to the life and evolution of a given science. To cite a recent example, radio astronomy did not emerge as the result of major innovations in the field of astronomy, nor was it motivated by internally generated quests and pressures. Similarly, modern computers were not developed to satisfy the computational needs of basic scientific research. In general, the technological innovations that have enormously increased the productive capacity of modern economies, through the spread of economical mass pro-

61

duction techniques, have also contributed greatly to experimental and observational natural sciences by generating new and powerful tools. But since such contributions are from an exogenous source, the new data and partial hypotheses that they generate are likely to raise a host of new problems that may not be solved for some time because the data are so new that they may not fit into the existing body of theory.

The development of economic analysis and research has been affected by stimuli provided, as in the experimental and observational natural sciences, not only by the unfolding of the internal logic and implications of some basic discoveries and theories, but also by the inflow of new data and emergence of new tools supplied exogenously, i.e., because of developments elsewhere. In particular, although the supply of primary data, which is provided largely by governments, *may* be affected by scholarly concern, it is usually generated by newly emerging interests reflecting either changed conditions or changed viewpoints, neither being necessarily the consequence of a new development within the structure of the economic discipline. The supply of both material and analytical tools—ranging from statistical techniques to mathematical devices for formal study of patterns and structures—may originate outside the field of economics, and for no reason connected with it. When such new data and tools appear, they may stimulate an accelerated pace of research within economics, resulting in a residue of unsolved problems until the findings have been fully integrated (which may take a long time).

In the field of economic and social research, major unsolved problems are always present—and not only because of the unexpected implications of an endoge-

62

nously stimulated investigation or because of the exogenously provided new data and tools. In the experimental
and observational natural sciences the exogenous additions relate to a universe with a long history of controlled observation and for which many interconnected,
widely tested generalizations have been established. And
in many of these sciences, the generalizations have been
firm enough to provide a basis for an effective material
technology, and for quite accurate predictions (as in the
case of astronomy). In the economics discipline, and
particularly in the study of economic growth of nations,
a field that seems to me to be central to the proper consideration of even short-term instabilities and relevant
policies, not only are there exogenously generated flows
of new data and tools that may represent a far greater
addition to a rather meager stock of data and tools than
is the situation in most experimental and observational
natural sciences. More important, variability of parameters and rapid changes in the aggregate magnitudes
and structural relations, are prevalent. This is because
the process of secular economic change is, at least in
modern economic growth, shaped by social and economic adjustments to a changing potential of technological advance, the latter in turn connected with the
continuous advance of basic science and other useful
knowledge. What happens is that an attempt is made to
analyze and generalize by using simplifying assumptions
that remove many major sources of possible change
(putting them into an exogenous pound). Although this
procedure may serve for some short-term problems and
in periods of moderate change (and not too safely even
then), it is soon confronted with major rapid changes in
economic conditions and structure, in the basic rules of

63

society concerning economic activity, and in accepted views concerning the limits of private and public economic policy. The conclusions must then be revised.

The history of economic analysis and research dealing with the broader aspects of economic growth, stability, and equity for national economies has been full of "surprises": major changes in technological bases of economic production—unforeseen, and hence not fully understood; successive inventions and innovations in institutional adjustment to basic changes in material conditions and in social judgments; revolutions in the political and social structures of a number of societies, particularly those now behind the Communist Iron Curtain, that have had considerable effect on the channeling and control of their economic growth and distribution processes. Indeed, many of the factors discussed above, in explaining the acceleration in the supply of primary data and greater concentration on economic measures and quantitative economic analysis, were direct results of these rather unexpected major changes within the older, more developed free market economies, as well as in the rest of the world. It is hardly a surprise that acceleration in the rate of inflow of new data, tools, and economic research tended to be associated with a large residue of unsolved problems—evidence of the substantial lag of effective economic research behind the rapid and variable course of growth and of accompanying structural changes in the several aspects of the national economy.

The responsiveness of economic research to major current changes, inevitably to the relative neglect of older and still not fully resolved problems, is understandable. Such major changes represent significant additions to economic experience; and since they are unexpected and not fully understood, questions naturally arise as to their bearing on the meaningfulness of extant economic measures and the validity of the available theoretical hypotheses. If the relevance of the accepted measures and hypotheses that the discipline had previously supplied is put into question by the new events, emphasis on the interpretation of the latter, in the light of existing knowledge, is inescapable. When the discipline provides no relevant acceptable hypotheses, it becomes imperative to generate some tentative explanation, if only to provide orientation for further exploration. If the changes carry with them some undesirable consequences, practical pressures are added to the purely intellectual pressures of contradiction between the new changes and past patterns, or of lacunae in any systematic basis for interpretation. In this case, delay in reaching better understanding might be costly: it might permit undesirable consequences to occur again; it might allow the costs to be distributed less than optimally; and it might delay or prevent the consensus that is needed for ameliorative action.

Given the limited resources, and the impact of these intellectual and practical pressures generated by major changes, it is not surprising that the focus of economic research shifts from one set of new changes to another in their succession in time. As the major depression of the 1930's deepened, most of the economic research effort was directed to it, to the neglect of earlier problems related to reparations and international transfers, reduction of immigration, local depressed industries, and the like. When we entered World War II, emphasis shifted to problems of economic mobilization and warfare, to the neglect of the major depression that had not yet been adequately studied or fully understood. And after World

65

War II, the problems of economic growth in this country and in other parts of the world, occasioned by inter-system competition and the special situation of the newly independent (and other) less developed countries, attracted much attention and generated a large volume of quantitative economic research. Within the past decade, interest appears to have shifted to urban problems and poverty, even though our understanding of the problems of economic growth is still tentative; and questions have been raised as to the meaningfulness of our measures of growth and as to the validity of the available hypotheses as bases for adequate analysis and considered policy.

Three implications of the preceding discussion bear directly upon our theme. The first relates to the reasons why many of the major changes in the national economy, in the course of its growth, come as surprises, that is, are not adequately foreseen by existing theory and knowledge. We stressed in this connection the characteristics of technological change that powers modern economic growth, and that calls for numerous adjustments by way of social innovations and changes in conditions of life. But technological change itself stems from progress in basic sciences and other accretions of useful knowledge. As it affects economic productivity, it also changes conditions of life and creates potentials for new types of demand which, in turn, stimulate technological change. Finally, the latter may provide new tools and insights for basic science and lead to further discoveries.

The sequence suggested is long. The many links, sequential and collateral, have differing slippage; and the sequence cannot be forecast without a thorough systematic and interrelated theory of all the processes in-

66

volved—the development of science, the level and direction of technological innovations, the course of the social innovations and changes in conditions of life emerging in the utilization of technological innovations, and so on. Yet such a long sequence is the substance of modern economic growth. Its combination with diverse historical heritages throughout the world, with which we are all too poorly acquainted (for reasons touched upon above), produced the surprises. In the older developed countries these surprises may lie in the unexpected character of the new technologies and of their social consequences—and partly in unforeseen changes in the rest of the world; in the less developed countries they may be the unexpected adjustments that societies make to their backwardness in response to the apparently huge potential of modern technologies—and partly to the unforeseen changes in the more developed countries.

The second implication, while really part of the first, should be separately noted. From the standpoint of the economics discipline, the difficulties with the long sequence suggested lie partly in the complex interweaving of economic processes with social and intellectual processes that are beyond the boundaries of economics no matter how broadly defined. If the forces that determine trends in basic science and in the accumulation of useful knowledge that provides an increasingly rich basis for technological change are somehow linked to economic processes, the linkages are still to be established. (Classical and Marxian economics resolved the problem by declaring technological advance too feeble, relative to other factors, to matter in the long run.) The linkage of changing technology, to changing scale of firm, to changing conditions of life is more within the scope of the

67

economic discipline. However, the sequence cannot be completed in analysis so long as technological change is treated as an exogenous variable, and so long as we lack the theoretical system that encompasses changes in tastes and in conditions of life as a corollary of changes in economic productivity. The point here is that the economic trends that we observe over the long periods have antecedents and consequences in social and intellectual processes. An economic trend between times t and $t +$ 50 is a result not only of economic events over the period (or before, i.e., in $t - 1$, $t - 2$, . . .) but also of the noneconomic antecedents and consequences of the economic events over the same period. If this is a true characterization of the interweaving of economic and other factors in the course of *economic* growth, analysis and data limited to the economic discipline can serve only if subjected to highly restrictive (and often unrealistic) assumptions as to the limits within which these noneconomic antecedents and consequences can act. And this may well be the reason why the discipline is now reaching out to extend its boundaries.

The third important implication is that the surprises contain not only a large positive element—increasing productivity and capacity—but almost inevitably some negative elements—either reducing welfare in, or affecting the security of, the national economy. Positive growth must have negative aspects in a world of independent and competing nations. The usually rapid advance of a major country may be viewed by others as a security threat that could not have been foreseen. More important, technological change, based on exploration and exploitation of the only partly known, and representing, in fact, manipulation of natural processes for human purposes, is likely to have undesirable effects. These cannot often be foreseen, because man deals here with much that is unknown and that is learned only with practice. For example, if modern technology is based on control of much more power than in the past, and requires highly durable producer goods to channel such power—with durability far exceeding anything known heretofore, including that of organic substances—can one fully foresee the consequence that indestructible residues of economically obsolete equipment would clutter the landscape? Or, when mass production of the automobile began, with its very low capacity of utilization and little pressure for efficient consumption of fuel, could one have foreseen the consequences in congestion and in pollution? Indeed, any major technological change that is necessarily a *disruptive* modification of nature for the benefit of man must, for this very reason, have *some* undesirable ecological consequences. Similar disfunctional elements can be attributed to any economic or social innovation, or even to any major modification of social ideology, that is, of the way people look at relations to each other and to nature. Although the modern corporation was a valuable legal organizational response to the requirements of modern, large-scale, capital-demanding technology, it lent itself to abuses in connection with attempts at monopolization; and one consequence of its development, not fully expected, was the separation of management from ownership, which created new problems. If the increased strength of nationalism was an ideological response to the organizational challenge provided by the enriching but disruptive potential of modern economic growth, some of its

69

negative consequences can hardly be denied; and many were not anticipated.

Regardless of such major consequences, the unexpected and undesirable aftermaths of the major technological changes and of many economic advances generate pressures for interpreting and measuring these changes and their corollaries in quantitative research dealing with economic growth. It is important to note that these pressures are not accidental, but are a continuous accompaniment of economic growth and change. Furthermore, the internal pressures may be the greater, the higher the rate of recent growth and the more marked the forays into the new and partly unknown reaches of technology and economic performance. The bearing upon the interpretive function of quantitative economic research is obvious.

Suggested Priorities

I have been referring to the study of economic growth in its broader quantitative aspects for several reasons: because I am more familiar with this field than with others; because I consider it central in that it provides a guiding framework for the study of its components and institutions; and because the National Bureau of Economic Research, which has contributed much in this area, should continue to play an important part in such research. But the association between an accelerated pace of research in recent decades and the variety of unsolved problems that remain is true not only of the broader field of economic growth of nations but also of many more specialized fields of research. Broad changes in the rate and structure of growth are likely to have reper-
70

cussions in all important sectors and institutions; changes in views on policy ramify from one field to others; the pressure to revise older notions concerning determining factors and limits of policy in special fields would presumably be affected by what happens in the economy at large.

To be sure, a major qualification is to be noted: the intensity of the impact discussed above need not, indeed cannot, be the same in all the subfields of economic analysis, for the pressures of major changes in conditions and outlook are not the same in all of them. The shifts of the limited research resources in the economics discipline from one set of problems to another, as we observe them over the longer-term past, are reflections of the unequal impact of the major changes in any given period. After all, we had no separate subdiscipline for the study of Communist economies in the 1920's or the 1930's, nor did we have courses on economic development in the graduate curricula; and monopoly and trust problems that loomed so large at one time in graduate teaching and research appear to have receded from the focus of attention. Even so, the variety of fields within which a high pace of quantitative research in the past was associated with many still unanswered problems is wide; and upon careful consideration, those currently neglected fields may prove deserving of more attention, especially if their possible contribution appears to be relevant to other research tasks. In trying to identify the major problems for research, one is thus left with the uncomfortable conclusion that the areas for quantitative research in which unsolved problems and promising further research loom large cover almost the full range of the economics discipline.

The last remark and the preceding discussion should suffice to convey my view on recent developments and problems in quantitative economic research, a view that reflects personal experience and judgment but perhaps for that reason leads to some specific priorities. This view, implicit in my emphasis on the broader aspects of national economies, suggests that, given the turbulent acceleration of economic research in recent decades, as well as the marked changes that have occurred in this country's economy and in the rest of the world since the mid-1940's, there is an obvious need for a wider and more critical synthesis of the many disparate measures and pieces of research into a coherent closely interrelated analysis of recent economic growth experience.

Such synthesis might well begin by concentrating on the post-World War II growth experience of this country—a quantitative analysis of its economic growth over the last twenty-five years, the sources of such growth, the structural changes and changes in conditions of life that accompanied it, the distribution of the gains from such growth, and the net balance of costs and returns. A major and comprehensive study would attempt to integrate all the partial studies and the analyses that have accumulated; it would widen the scope to include such basic aspects of economic growth as growth of population and its shifting distribution, technological changes in production and consumption, a critical scrutiny of the aggregative measures for hidden costs and returns and of concealed duplication and biased weighting, and a thorough examination of the distributive aspects of the process. The need for such a study is suggested by recent discussions—not only scholarly probings into the new aspects stimulated by "puzzles," but also widespread (or at least voluble) concern with the quality of our economic growth, and with the deficiencies of the national product measures as indicators of national progress.[9]

Such a broad topic may involve a whole series of studies rather than a single exploration—studies ranging from a technical examination of current measures, the problems in establishing the contributions of various factors to growth, possible revisions of the currently accepted sectoral classifications, deeper analysis of the income distribution, and the like, to the necessarily broader and more general issues raised by some of the problematic consequences of economic growth, or by the whole network of relations between economic growth and changes in the noneconomic aspects of the performance and structure of society at large. Although this may well be the case, we hope that a realization of the wide scope of the topic does not lead to its postponement as too ambitious, or to plans that are overly long-term. The suggestion advanced here cannot be taken to represent a well-thought-out program; this would be out of place.

[9] Much of the discussion in recent annual reports of the National Bureau (see, in particular, the paper by F. Thomas Juster in the *50th Annual Report,* September 1970, pp. 8–24) and in the colloquia papers by Professors Schultz, and Nordhaus and Tobin (Theodore W. Schultz, "Human Capital: Policy Issues and Research Opportunities," in *Economic Research: Retrospect and Prospect, Vol. VI, Human Resources;* and James Tobin and William D. Nordhaus, "Is Growth Obsolete?" *ibid., Vol. V, Economic Growth*), supports this impression of a need for critical revision of the current national economic accounts. The papers presented at a recent Conference on Income and Wealth (in Princeton, November 4–6, 1971) on the broad theme of Measurement of Economic and Social Performance strengthen this impression. One should stress that the dissatisfaction with the current national product measures is with their validity as gauges of economic growth, rather than as indexes of short-term changes in current economic performance.

The program should be a product of collective judgment and experience. But three aspects of the proposed topic, or complex of studies, seem to me to deserve recognition and further consideration.

The first is the emphasis on growth, i.e., sustained, nonreversible, major changes over a sufficiently long period to indicate the persistence of underlying forces, with short-term changes and instabilities treated as part of a longer process. Much of the recent quantitative economic research, particularly that initiated or stimulated by government, has been concentrated on the year-to-year changes that affect current government and private policy. As a result, the longer growth perspective has often been ignored; and changes over a year or two have been characterized as growth, although they may have contained a transitory component large enough, relative to the secular, to obscure the long-term movement. We badly need a longer perspective. Awareness of this has led to much criticism, in recent years, of the deficiencies of many current measures, despite the fact that they may be quite adequate, perhaps are the best, for short-term changes and problems. Indeed, that may be the very reason for their inadequacy in gauging the far greater transformations that occur over the longer period associated with growth. In widening the historical perspective, observation and analysis of some of the changes may have to be extended into the prewar period; and for many of these, the current study by Moses Abramovitz and Paul David, now nearing completion, should provide an important contribution.[10] But one

[10] This study of post-World War II growth in the United States in the light of the longer historical perspective is part of a cooperative project of similar studies for a number of developed countries, includ-

would hope that concentration on the post-World War II decades, with only limited and broad reference to the longer past, might permit a more intensive analysis, if only because of the greater stock of economic measures and partial analytical studies relating to the more recent period that have accumulated.

Second, the emphasis is on the growth of the national economy and those of its parts and components that should be distinguished for several analytical reasons. Such an emphasis should shed light on the sources of growth, on the shifts in relative shares of various groups and changes in the conditions of life required by participation in economic activity, on the burdens imposed and returns bestowed on the different groups in the community, on the dependence of the country's economy on others, either in the way of trade or of security, and the like. This combination of comprehensiveness, of aggregation that would strike the net balance of costs and returns in terms of socially accepted assumptions and knowledge, with analytically oriented disaggregation and scrutiny of differences in movement and relations among significant components, is of the essence in this complex of studies. And it is required if the study is to accomplish its two most important functions. It must establish a greater consensus on what happened, and what the implications are—a task particularly important in a democracy in which such consensus is a prerequisite for intelligent action (necessary, if not sufficient). It must organize the unrelated studies of specific aspects of

ing the United States, several European countries, and Japan. The project was initiated under the auspices of the Committee on Economic Growth of the Social Science Research Council in 1964 (see Social Science Research Council, *Annual Report, 1967–1968*).

the economy in order to provide a better orientation for economic analysis, aiming at better generalization on and better prediction (or at least foresight) of long-term trends.

Third, the aspects of economic and social change that should be included in such an analysis of post-World War II economic growth and its implications should reach beyond the economic, as defined in economic research. The growth processes, as indicated, involve a complicated interplay between trends in economic production and distribution proper, the growth of population and its adjustment to economic stimuli and to broader factors in life, changes in prevailing attitudes, the search for new knowledge and innovations, and the very structure of the "rest of the world." Consequently, greater understanding and more fruitful analysis call for extension of primarily economic research to cover at least the quantitative aspects of closely related social trends— in population numbers, in family life cycles, in bases for social stratification, in the specialized but highly crucial institutions concerned with basic and applied research and technological change, and so on. How far the extension should be pushed is a question that can be answered only in the course of formulating the program of such a study. Moreover, the answer will change as the study progresses and as the results of such extension cumulate. But the probings that have already been made—many are reported in recent National Bureau annual reports and others are evident in recent work on quantitative social indicators—suggest that we should *begin* with a broader view of the ramifications of economic growth processes than has been held in the great majority (indeed almost all) of economic research studies in the field.

76

Since the suggested study is aimed at quantitative analysis of the economic growth of this country since the mid-1940's, the sources and consequences, the social concomitants and the costs and returns to the living members of society, it can hardly be undertaken either by the government or by one or two individual scholars within the universities. The government, as already suggested, must, of necessity, concentrate on the day-to-day or year-to-year problems; and it is highly revealing that we have the annual *Economic Report of the President,* but no decennial or generational reports. Even if such reviews were to be initiated by the government, and this may happen if government assumes more direct and active policy responsibility for longer-term patterns of growth, it would require substantial pioneering work by scholars and analysts outside of the government to establish a consensus as to the most meaningful measures and their interrelations. This would, in fact, be one of the contributions of the complex of studies urged here. Nor can such a complex of studies, given its scope and the need to draw upon a variety of expertise and upon a large body of data, be effectively brought to completion by one or even several individual scholars. Only a research institute, with a wide background of experience in collective, quantitative research, could provide effective auspices and leadership.

If such a complex of studies were to be considered a priority item on the program of the National Bureau, it would have to draft some resources now used in more narrowly defined, more specific studies that promise to yield concrete results in the proximate future. This, of course, is the inevitable cost of far-flung, synthetic, broadly interpretive types of investigation that may

77

result in valuable revisions of simplistic notions, a better orientation, and better directions for future research, but may yield no specific findings of immediate value. Is the price too high? After all, the careful study of a single institution, e.g., the over-the-counter securities markets or the residential construction industry, will bring to light some elements of irrationality or of wasteful practices, and the needed policy changes. Even wider but still fairly specific subjects for quantitative economic analysis are numerous and come easily to mind. And yet I would argue that the long-term yield of the broad investigation is very high in terms of additions to tested knowledge and the provision of a better basis for consensus on the goals of the economy and society and related judgments of recent major changes. Furthermore, a broader study of the type suggested provides a unifying focus for a research institute like the National Bureau. It is interesting that upon the 25th anniversary of the National Bureau, Wesley C. Mitchell stressed "national income as an incitement to and a framework for other studies." [11] In a sense I am repeating Dr. Mitchell's emphasis on the possible contribution of the suggested study to the guidance and unification of the National Bureau's research program. The one modification that I make is to stress the use of national income measures as gauges of economic growth, rather than as indexes of short-term changes.

Finally, it may be argued that some specific economic problems calling for relevant quantitative economic research are more urgent than a broad analysis of economic

[11] Wesley C. Mitchell, *The National Bureau's First Quarter-Century*, Twenty-Fifth Annual Report of the National Bureau of Economic Research, New York, May 1945, p. 20.

78

growth since World War II. Examples abound and we mention a few: the persistence of poverty and welfare problems; the plight of the cities, particularly the central cores of metropolitan areas; the ever-present national security and international tensions. And, as already indicated, it cannot be denied that new problems arise continuously and exert pressure for response in research and policy. Yet it seems to me that many of these problems must be seen within a wider framework and perspective; that continuity in economic and social research would provide a base from which the succession of ever-changing problems could be better understood; and that it is the task of scholarship to provide this broader base for interpretation, generalization, and policy analysis. We must have centers for research that are devoted to these broader views and the wider issues that they raise, without being forced to succumb to the continuous pressure of ever-changing crises and urgent problems of the year, or even the decade. That very rapid succession of urgent problems is in itself evidence of the need for a broader base and wider perspective. If, in the 1920's and the 1930's, people in the developed countries could be concerned about the sluggish population growth, and a generation later were at the peak of excitement about the menace of rapid population growth; if in one period there is worry about surplus of savings and lack of investment opportunities, and in another about a critical shortage of capital funds; if in one period demand is keen for higher education as the proper preparation for a productive life, and in another its relevance is questioned—then the need for a wider perspective and broader base seems clear. Needless to say, the re-evaluation of past experience and current

79

problems within this wider context is a task that requires the employment of research talent and experience on a consistent and systematic basis.

The priority that might be given to this broad study or complex of studies in the program of the National Bureau would not represent much of a departure from past experience. Without considering questions of organization, planning, etc. (which would be out of place here), one could argue that such a study is feasible under the auspices of the National Bureau. It is squarely within its tradition of contributing to the understanding of basic quantitative aspects of the performnace of the economy and society in this country.

Another broad topic that seems to me to deserve high priority in any consideration of quantitative economic research is not quite within that tradition; and raises some major difficulties for which no ready answer is apparent. This topic is the badly needed analysis of economic growth experience and problems in other countries. The dangers of limiting research and analysis of economic growth problems to a single country are too obvious to need stressing. Yet one gets the impression that the accelerated pace of quantitative economic research and the improvement in its tools have resulted in a concentration of scholarly research on the single country of which the scholar is a resident that is greater now than in the past. Even if this impression is wrong, it is a fact that there is a short supply of sustained quantitative economic research utilizing comparisons of the growth experience of several countries—comparisons that might shed some light on the growth experience of countries in which native economic research is limited or almost non-existent, as is true of many Communist and of most less developed countries. I would place a high value on comparative research because it would provide a better analysis, a better identification of the invariant and variant elements, and a better basis for interpretation, generalization, and policy treatment. Considered interpretation of the "rest of the world" would better the understanding of the position of one's country vis-à-vis others. And it is crucial for the formation of a social consensus, particularly in democracies, based on wider world intelligence and not on ignorant self-centered provincialism. Greater knowledge of foreign economies and societies is indispensable if more intelligent public policy bearing on international relations is to emerge. One hesitates to pass judgment, but it is conceivable that some of the current problems of the economy of this country are linked to limited understanding of other economies and societies.

I do not mean to suggest that there have not been recent valuable accretions of new data, economic measures, and quantitative economic research for other countries. These, in fact, have permitted comparative studies of a scope and solidity of empirical foundation unattainable in the past. The National Bureau's own research program has included studies of international migration, a series of studies on the economy of the USSR, and some scattered studies of other countries. Several branches of the government provide immensely valuable series of statistical studies on population and labor force, agricultural output, mineral resources, and labor conditions in other countries. Congressional committees are responsible for special hearings that mobilize large amounts of information on selected parts of the world (particularly the major Communist countries). A profusion of studies of economic growth experience and problems in a variety of countries has also been published by scholars in this and other developed countries. The compilation of comparable data for a large body of nations and the series of monographic studies of various problems by the international agencies, including some regional branches of the United Nations, have greatly enriched our knowledge of economic growth patterns and problems in many parts of the world.

However, much of the research is episodic; far too much of it is produced either on an ad hoc basis or as a corollary of the functioning of international agencies (or, sometimes, of domestic government agencies concerned with foreign areas). We lack a sustained scholarly effort that would apply to the study of other areas of the world the criteria that an economist in a developed country applies to research bearing on his own country—criteria such as data adequacy, relevant economic measures, and the greater understanding of the institutional and social framework within which economic growth and performance take place. These desiderata are most easily met in comparative studies of free market developed countries, particularly those affiliated with Western European civilization—although even here misunderstanding and lack of comprehension are possible because proper appraisal of the specific institutional conditions and of the quality of the relevant data is difficult. And, of course, great assistance is rendered to a research scholar in one developed country by equally competent research scholars in the others. But difficulties arise when, as in the case of Japan, the developed country has long historical roots in a civilization that developed apart from the Western European for millennia before the late nineteenth century. The difficulties are greatly com-

82

pounded for the Communist countries, with their distinctive political and institutional structures and their limitations on critically and objectively oriented native economic and social science scholarship. In any one of the less developed countries the paucity of primary data, the irrelevance of some "standard" economic measures (formulated primarily for developed economies), and the scarcity of native scholars severely limit the contribution of domestic scholarship and data to quantitative analysis of that country's growth experience, and magnify the difficulties of adequate comprehension and analysis by research economists from the developed countries. Because of the absence of sustained, continuous, and cumulative quantitative economic research on areas other than that in which the scholar resides, little research is now being done on the "difficult" areas, and much of that is of poor quality. Shoddiness of data untested by adequate analysis often renders the estimates that appear in international compendia highly dubious. And many of the studies, geared toward pressing policy problems and emphasizing various "gaps" and "bottlenecks," are dogmatic, simplistic over-generalizations because of inadequate empirical bases.

The difficulties of stimulating sustained economic research concerning other areas, research that would produce results useful for comparative studies and proper orientation in this rapidly changing world, cannot be explored here. We are all familiar with the disciplinary structure of economics within the academic institutions and with the difficulties a scholar encounters in fully understanding the specific complexities of another country —particularly when he deals with less developed countries or areas outside the sources of Western scholarship.

83

No extra-university, academic centers exist that would provide the proper conditions and facilities for this type of quantitative analysis of foreign economies. To be sure, area study centers are attached to several universities, but their difficulties in attracting economic scholars and maintaining continuity are formidable and well known.

In short, there has never been a "Bureau of Economic Research" in the field of quantitative economic research bearing on foreign economies, one that would concentrate on a continuous and cumulative program dealing with the basic quantitative framework of these other national economies and thus assuring some minimum standards of quantitative analysis. A few *national* bureaus, or their equivalents, have been established in some developed countries; but most other parts of the world have no such centers for quantitative research. And for various reasons the international agencies that have burgeoned since World War II do not provide the conditions for development of continuous economic research, despite the distribution of an enormous quantity of data and the publication of a variety of reports. The former are often of rather variable quality and dubious relevance, and the latter are often ad hoc studies, not always free from the limitations imposed by the need to maintain international courtesy or to respond to regional interests.

The range of the studies comprised in this second topic is far wider than that implied in the study of post-World War II economic growth of this country. Any considered discussion of its feasibility would involve problems of area grouping, limits within which comparative study would seem worthwhile, variety of criteria involved in selecting one or another area and type of economy for intensive study, and the like. I am not prepared to en-

gage in such discussion; nor is it relevant on this occasion. But it seems to me that the broader interests of the
economics discipline and the requirement that economic
research provide a better basis for social consensus demand a more sustained effort to introduce continuity
and higher standards in quantitative research on many
important areas of the world—particularly those outside
the free market developed countries. Since, on this jubi-
lee occasion, we should be receptive to all research pro-
posals—even of almost impossibly difficult tasks—and
since the National Bureau has engaged from time to time
in quantitative research on foreign areas, I thought it not
improper to suggest the priority of the task and the need
to consider the possibility of securing continuity and
higher standards of empirical research in these areas.

What could be done in response to the need, if its
priority is recognized, is not clear to me at present; and
it is even less clear whether the National Bureau can
play an important substantive role. One would have to
know more about the research under way in the area
centers attached to the universities in this and other
developed countries; take stock of the various comparative studies recently completed or under way, whether by
academic scholars or in research branches of international agencies and organizations; and think through the
role that an institution like the National Bureau could
play, and at what cost. As already indicated, this review
and stock-taking would have to be done against a background of fairly clear notions of the method by which
the vast field of "rest of the world" should be subdivided,
and of the most relevant criteria of choice of areas and
of the most urgent problems that need comparative
analysis. An organized discussion of the comparative

study of economic growth and structure, conducted under the auspices of the National Bureau in 1958, resulted in several suggestions on research objectives and organization.[12] But no substantive program followed this effort at preliminary exploration.

My own judgment is that study of the growth experience and problems in at least some selected economies would prove valuable. A review of the field would, it is hoped, show whether and how the National Bureau can contribute to stimulating and developing more consistent, continuous quantitative research, at higher standards, in the important area of comparative economic growth and structure.

5. SUMMARY

In summarizing the paper, I begin with the distinction that was drawn between the ever-present conditions of quantitative economic research, and the particular situation in the field in the early 1970's.

As to the former, I noted five sets of conditions. The first was the origin and supply of the primary data. They are provided by the active economic agents themselves—individuals, firms, agencies, etc.—and economists have no direct control over their supply. Consequently, the quality of the data varies, there are lacunae in the available stock, and the supply of the data lags behind the emergence of the problems upon which they are to shed light.

The second condition was the dependence of economic measures—for which the primary data are the

[12] See *The Comparative Study of Economic Growth and Structure: Suggestions on Research Objectives and Organization,* National Bureau of Economic Research, Exploratory Report 4, New York, 1959.

raw material—upon economic theory and the broader social philosophy within which it is embedded. Consequently, differences or changes in the broader philosophy, and in the theories of production, prices, and welfare, yield different economic measures for the same country and the same time. Economic measurement derives meaning only from the underlying assumptions and the relevant theoretical framework. It is implicitly a test of these assumptions and theories; and, if it produces changes in them, it must in turn be revised.

Third, at least within the period of modern economic growth (the last 150 to 200 years), the quantitative framework and the relations within and among the national economies have undergone major and rapid changes. These can be ascribed to the rapid growth in the stock of useful knowledge and the institutional and ideological adjustments to it. Because of these changes, the task of quantitative economic research in identifying the persistent and predictable elements and distinguishing them from the transient and historically accidental is made all the more difficult.

Fourth, the concentration of economic research on the scholar's own country is clearly associated with the easier accessibility of data, greater knowledge of underlying conditions, and, particularly, more intensive pressures for economic analysis of domestic problems— pressures originating within the nation's society and government and coupled with an available channel for applying analysis to policy. Yet, more systematic study on a comparative basis (in addition to the already developed study of international economic flows) is required to provide a sounder basis for generalizations and more intelligent consensus regarding the country's

87

role vis-à-vis the rest of the world. Such study is quite limited, given the preponderant absorption of scholarly resources in domestic economic trends and problems, and the immense difficulties of making comparative studies that meet minimum standards.

Fifth, and finally, economic processes are closely interwoven with other social processes. Particularly in growth experience, the long sequence of economic impulse, a noneconomic response (say by a political or demographic process), followed by an economic change, is typical. Consequently, the interpretation of economic measures may require not only economic analysis but also consideration of the relevant framework of related social sciences and other disciplines. In fact, the very boundary between economic and other analysis may shift over time and from problem to problem.

These conditions of quantitative economic research were illustrated primarily by reference to the study of the economic growth of nations. But they apply, with differing weight, to research relating to the sectoral or any other aspect of national economies; to short-term changes as well as secular trends; to historical interpretation, theoretical investigation, or policy analysis—whenever these employ, as they must, observational, quantitative data. These conditions were presented, perhaps naturally, as impediments to research designed to yield generalizations sufficiently specific and firm to provide a basis for meaningful prediction and for discriminating policy evaluation. But they should also be viewed as challenges, resulting from the tension between what existing theory demands or implies and what the observable and changeable reality reveals.

Three implications of the conditions just summarized

are directly relevant to the role of a research institution like the National Bureau. First, given the origin and supply of the primary data, and the importance of government in the collection, organization, and, recently, analysis of economic statistics, on the one hand, and the difficulties of carrying on sustained, large-scale quantitative research within the framework of university departments, on the other hand, there is a clear need for economic research institutes. Such organizations should be able to handle the broader quantitative research problems on a continuing and collective basis, unaffected either by the pressures of governmental concerns or by the limitations necessarily imposed by attachment to a single university. Second, since quantitative economic research must deal with the ever-emerging new (and mostly unforeseen) changes in the economy and society and must interpret them in the light of existing knowledge, the process of measurement and interpretation is important for both theoretical analysis and the broader orientation of society. The nongovernmental, public research institute is not only a research laboratory for the specialist but also, in a way, a finder and keeper of truth for society at large, a producer of tested and acceptable measures, and a source of the balanced evaluation and judgment that should facilitate social consensus. Third, more thought must be devoted to the organizational problems of quantitative economic research that goes beyond the scope of this country's economy, and aims at comparative analysis and wider orientation. In an increasingly interdependent world, the intellectual and social costs of inadequate knowledge of the rest of the world are increasingly heavy.

As regards the present situation in the field, particularly the quantitative study of economic growth—its

89

magnitude, structure, time pattern, and equity, for national economies—I can only offer broad impressions; but they may also be relevant to economic research in other fields.

The foremost impression is of a striking acceleration in the quantitative study of economic growth—in the supply of primary data, in the generation of aggregative and disaggregated economic measures, in attempts at interpretive analysis, and in the formulation of hypotheses, ranging from simple historical generalizations to elaborate mathematical models of imaginatively conceived (and imaginary) economic growth processes. This explosive outburst in the last two to two-and-a-half decades, coming after a century of almost total neglect, was associated with the assumption of greater responsibility by governments, particularly in the developed free market economies, for economic growth and employment; and in the international intersystem competition, with their greater concern for the economic growth of the less developed countries. This acceleration, as reflected in numbers of economists and the volume of publications, appears to have been true of economic research at large; and the same can be said for other social science disciplines (at least in this country).

Much has surely been learned; a vast stock of relevant economic measures has accumulated; the inventory of relatively firm empirical findings has grown; and a host of theoretical hypotheses has been advanced, many of them, however, too simple and partial to be valid without major and, lacking wider study, unspecifiable qualifications. Older theories have been found wanting, and attempts have been made to bridge the gap of ignorance revealed when the old theories were confronted

90

with the newly secured data and findings. The very discrediting of old theories was an advance, in that it removed constraints on policy choices. Emphasis has shifted rapidly from one presumptively crucial source of economic growth to another—not only in the rationale underlying international aid efforts, but also in the scholarly literature. And, it should be particularly stressed, the post-World War II record of economic growth of nations is most impressive, despite the breakdowns in some less developed countries where the search for national unity or for adequate internal equity has not been successful. High aggregate growth rates have been attained; the developed economies have been relatively free from major cyclical downturns, and have moved ahead toward economic equality. The rate of this economic advance in most parts of the world was much faster than in the pre-World War II, or even pre-World War I period. It was in shining contrast to developments in the two decades following World War I; and, one may suggest, far exceeded economic expectations entertained, at least in this country and most probably elsewhere, immediately after World War II (however disappointing the contrast between expectation and reality in the fields of international comity and peace).

But we are still far from a tested theory of economic growth, an aim that we may never quite realize. Many questions remain that demand intensive exploration and at least provisional answers as necessary elements in even a tentative understanding of the growth process. A record of successful economic performance is not necessarily evidence that we understand the process. Nor is rapid economic growth, even if accompanied by greater stability and wider equity, without consequences that

91

may be viewed by contemporaries as urgent problems—
even if they are, in a broader historical perspective, far
less weighty than past problems resolved (or minimized)
by past growth. In short, quantitative research in the
field of economic growth is today, and will continue to
be, under the double pressure of questions raised by new
or newly studied experience and of policy problems generated by some consequences (frequently unforeseen, or,
if foreseen, often unprevented) of recent growth. Paradoxically, the number of questions and the variety of
what may be seen as policy problems may be greater
after a period of accelerated study and growth than in
the "good old" days when both study and growth were
relatively stagnant. In those days, economic growth was
viewed as a process much beyond the control of man,
and its low rate did not produce the unsettling impact of
rapid structural changes. The relation between the recent developments in the study and process of economic
growth may have a parallel in the relation between the
developments in the study and process of change of
many economic sectors and institutions.

Selection of problems for quantitative research requires an effort to take stock, similar to that made in
other National Bureau anniversary colloquia,[13] but it is
not attempted here because of the unmanageably wide
scope of the field. Questions bearing upon the quality
and causes, the why and the wherefore, of economic
growth of nations will, in all likelihood, continue to
loom large in the scholarly and public mind. The need
for a wider historical and analytical perspective is obvious. It is not clear that the search for such a perspec-

[13] See pp. vii–x for a listing of these colloquia.

tive and a more sustained and objective study should concentrate on economic processes. There are other aspects of social structure and performance, which, at least at first glance, seem to lag behind in their capacity to adjust to technological and economic advance. But there are enough economic problems in the growth and changing structure of this and other nations to demand continuous and wider effort by research institutions like the National Bureau. The Bureau should, as in the past, deal with the basic measures of this country's economic performance. It should make an effort to have these measures reflect the changing reality and give meaning to the changes within the analytical framework of our discipline, or of that part of it that may still be relevant and at least partly valid. And the National Bureau should also consider the possibility of applying its experience and tools more widely and systematically to comparative measurement and analysis of the economic performance of nations.